About the Author

Loring Gimbel was an English teacher who took on the challenge of educating patients at two large medical centers in Calgary, Canada for over 25 years. Since he knew how to communicate clearly and how to implement learning strategies, he succeeded in finding ways to empower patients with medical knowledge to help them effectively participate in their care.

He passionately believes that education is integral to health care since minds and bodies work in sync for healing. In this book, he concisely gives you his best insight on how to educate and achieve amazing results, from improving outcomes to creating efficiencies to save time and money. Patients and professionals can benefit exponentially.

In addition to specialising in patient education, Loring loves to travel so much that he has explored 49 American states and 64 countries! His adventures and experiences have given him insight into the best of life around the globe, as reflected in the international appeal of this book. He wishes you the real rewards of caring interaction, learning, educating, and healing for the utmost in wellness of mind and body.

Loring Gimbel

How to Educate and Empower Your Patients

AUSTIN MACAULEY PUBLISHERS™

LONDON • CAMBRIDGE • NEW YORK • SHARJAH

A CIP catalogue record for this title is available from the British Library.

ISBN 9781788788731 (Paperback)
ISBN 9781786128614 (E-Book)
www.austinmacauley.com

First Published (2017)
Austin Macauley Publishers Ltd.
25 Canada Square
Canary Wharf
London
E14 5LQ

Acknowledgements

Even though I was an educator for over 25 years, I was even more of a learner during the whole time. I needed to continually learn about the real needs of patients and how to help them gain essential knowledge. I needed to learn what it was like to experience their conditions, their confusion, their stress, and their desire to be empowered with clear and practical information to help them heal. I needed to see how education can make a profound difference in their coping, their participation, and their health outcomes. I'd like to thank the thousands of patients who taught me what the "guts" of education is all about.

I'd also like to thank the hundreds of professionals who presented to me, who clarified concepts for me, who worked with me to educate patients in multiple initiatives, and who inspired me with your ideas and caring approaches. The process of educating patients always requires a team, and I greatly appreciate your willingness, your hard work, and your expertise in all the ways we connected and collaborated.

I especially want to thank four outstanding professionals for your help in preparing this book. You clarified references for me, you edited my drafts, you offered objective viewpoints, you made valuable suggestions, and you encouraged me. Thank you very much for your willingness to contribute your valuable time, knowledge, and talents to refining and enhancing this book.

Louise Watson, BScN, Alberta Health Services

Yongtao Lin, MLIS, Alberta Health Services

Dave Whiteside, BN (Nursing), BA (Linguistics),
Alberta Health Services

Kerry Harwood, RN, MSN,
Director, Advanced Practice
Former Director, Cancer Patient Education Program
Duke University Hospital

Table of Contents

Introduction

To live well we need healthy bodies, but we are surrounded by threats to our wellbeing. In recent decades, medical research has advanced our ability to manage and resolve our injuries and diseases. But every step of progress seems to be counterbalanced by increasing challenges such as overwhelming needs and demands, an increase in both young and aging populations, and desperately limited resources.

Educating patients is a powerful and effective way to enhance health care and reduce these challenges. We live in an era of enlightenment and empowerment. Just like increasing knowledge benefits how well we function in life, so educating patients empowers them to actively and effectively participate in their care. This empowerment has profound benefits to them as well as to health care providers and medical centers. I've written this book to explain the key role of education in health care. I offer you extensive insight and targeted strategies on how to educate your patients well.

I have worked to educate patients in medical centers for over 25 years in the fields of ophthalmology and oncology. I've also attended and participated in several patient education conferences at leading institutions such as the Mayo Clinic in Rochester, Minnesota; Princess Margaret Hospital in Toronto; Memorial Sloan Kettering Cancer Center in New York City; MD Anderson Cancer Center in Houston; and the University of Michigan in Ann Arbor. For many years, I also participated on the boards of two health organizations that exist to support patients.

Through my education, experience, connections, and engagement with thousands of patients, I've learned a lot about what patients want to know and need to know. I've also learned much about how they learn, and what types of learning options work well. I know the big difference that effective education can make in the lives of patients to improve outcomes and reduce costs.

The purpose of this book is to offer you a volume of practical information that you can use right away in your roles as health care providers. This book is not a summary of research about patient education. I have reviewed much of the research and heard it presented at multiple conferences to confirm that my concepts are based on solid ground. If you conduct literature searches of medical education journals, you will find these studies that confirm what I'm advocating here. But I've also reached beyond what formal research has so far revealed to show you a vision of the profound effects that education can offer. I challenge you to further prove that these concepts and strategies absolutely work as you track the patterns of evidence in your patients and in the function of your medical centers.

Each chapter in this book works as an important independent unit, so don't feel that you need to read it progressively from beginning to end. This is a detailed guide with each chapter supporting the concepts of the others as they all work together to reveal dynamic education initiatives and the strategies to make them happen. Read and use each part of this book as it relates to your patient interactions, your interests, your leadership, your caring, and your goals.

Educating your patients is the key to getting all of their dimensions working together, along with you, for the best possible outcomes of health and life. I wish you success as you employ your expertise to this essential process of enlightenment and empowerment.

Loring Gimbel, MA, BA
Patient Education Specialist

It's Your Story Too

As a health care provider, your work and life is an unfolding story, and your decisions affect the plot line. You want to be a great character and an effective healer who is liked and respected by patients and peers. You want to offer information and treatments that benefit the lives of many patients. You may want to be a hero who makes discoveries, demonstrates integrity, raises standards, and leaves an admirable legacy. You want to make others healthy and happy. You want your story to be an inspiration to those who connect with you now, and for those who will follow you later.

You can make your story better by interacting well with the stories of your patients. So, connect with the real lives of your patients, engage with them and educate them in relation to their minds, emotions, and spirits, as well as their bodies. When you enlighten your patients, you empower them to actively and effectively participate in their care, which often leads to higher satisfaction and better outcomes. Keep your own story in mind as you play a leading character in the stories of your patients.

From the chapter in this book called
How to Use Stores to Educate Patients

The Power of
Patient Education

The Connection Between Minds and Bodies

Our brains and bodies are interconnected and dependent on each other to function. Brains are complex networks of circuits and systems that regulate, manage, and control our bodies. While much of this control is autonomic, a great deal can be directed by our knowledge, desires, and conscious choices.

Input to our brains can cause instant reactions in our bodies, such as an increased heartbeat and a flight from fear. Other input to our brains can increase our stress and negatively impact our bodies. What we learn in our minds about the profound effect of lifestyle choices on our physical health can encourage us to make positive changes that benefit our bodies. When we learn the facts about our medical conditions and treatments, we are much better equipped to respond by playing an active role in dealing with the problems.

Of course, what happens in our bodies also affects our brains. An unhealthy body can lead to impaired brain function. Poor blood flow in our bodies usually means poor circulation to our brains as well, so heart attacks and strokes are results of similar blood flow problems. Physical pain also impairs our mental ability to focus and function. Therefore educating minds to help bodies can also boost the ability of bodies to help brains by providing a healthy context for optimal functioning.

Effective patient education is essential to quality health care since it affects the wellbeing and outcomes of your patients. It also affects your success in treating them, your reputation as a care provider, and the whole process of care at medical centers. If you want to treat your patients' bodies effectively, you must also educate their minds to collaborate on this multi-dimensional journey to health.

The Real Benefits of Educating Your Patients

Helps sync brains and bodies – Since minds and bodies work in continual collaboration with each other, the minds of educated patients can work much better to help their bodies deal with health challenges. Educated patients know the framework of facts about their problems and treatments, so they are able to act and interact in supportive ways. Apart from conscious choices, a mind that is in sync with the body's problems and treatments will naturally help the body respond more effectively, as demonstrated by the placebo effect and other evidence.

Keeps focus on reality – When patients have their health issues and treatments clearly explained to them, they are then in a position to deal with this reality, whether it is encouraging or not. If patients have not been well informed, the resulting gaps and misconceptions may cause them to try dealing with false information or imaginary scenarios rather than their real conditions.

Helps regulate emotional response – Feelings follow thoughts, so when your patients have accurate information in their minds, their emotions tend to respond more appropriately. Lack of information leaves gaps that the emotions tend to fill in with unwarranted fears and other misdirected feelings. When the emotions of your patients respond to the real facts, they can also become effectively engaged in the healing process. In turn, their social and spiritual natures can also respond and engage with the real situation. So, patient education plays a leading role in getting all of their human dimensions working together for health.

Reduces stress – Lack of knowledge, the resulting confusion, and a vivid imagination are at the center of much patient stress. When patients have been well informed, most tend to have less stress because they usually deal better with the real situation than with the confusion and fears of what they don't understand.

Empowers patients to participate – When patients are enlightened, they are also empowered to actively and effectively participate in the process of their care. Taking on this informed and active role can dramatically affect their response to treatments and the success of reaching the highest goals for their wellbeing.

Increases sense of value – Patients have a greater sense of value when you provide them with effective education. They realize they are being treated as intelligent human beings with a right to understand and participate rather than just bodies that need fixing. When you show them you believe that education will help them, they'll tend to believe it as well.

Helps form partnership for care – Most patients want to understand their medical conditions so they can work along with you in dealing with them. This partnership has many benefits, and it lies at the foundation of mutual understanding, trust, empathy, collaboration, and healing. With effective education, patients realize they are partners with you in their care. They see how they and their health care team can communicate and work together for the best possible outcomes.

Enhances consultations – When patients are educated about their conditions and treatments, they have the understanding to discuss their health issues intelligently with their care team. Informed patients are better able to understand further medical explanations, ask directed questions, trust the recommendations of the providers, and make informed decisions. Because they feel that they have communicated effectively, they also tend to be happier with their consultations and care.

Inspires confidence in you – When you take the time and make the effort to help patients understand what is happening with their bodies and how treatments work to resolve these problems, they tend to have more confidence in you. With everything they read and hear, they don't automatically trust the decisions of health care providers. But when you clearly explain things to them, they know that you understand their health problems and are working to provide the best solutions.

Helps clarify your evidence-based approach – Patients often read and hear information that is not based on objective evidence, so they may come to you confused about their diagnosis and possible treatments. They may expect or request treatments that are not based on reliable research. Patients need help to distinguish reliable information from that which is not. Clear explanations, materials, and programs can help convince them of the importance of being evidence-based and can direct them in their knowledge searches.

Clarifies treatment options – When patients have two or more options for treatment, they need to be clearly informed so they are empowered to make wise decisions. With clarity, patients are able to make the choices that will best meet their health objectives, within the scope of what is possible.

Encourages adherence – When patients understand the importance and powerful influence of their roles, they are much more likely to adhere and do such things as show up for their appointments, take their meds, and make life-style changes.

Increases satisfaction – Patients tend to be more satisfied with their care when they have been educated by their health care providers, especially when they have had the chance to ask questions and get clear answers. With this communication they sense that they have been understood, and they understand better too. They feel that they have connected constructively and well.

Helps define roles – Informative discussion can clarify the roles of health care providers, patients, and family members in dealing with health issues. Since much of the care is provided by patients and families themselves, it is essential that they know their specific roles and feel informed and confident enough to participate.

Helps align the support of family members – Education is also important for the supportive relationships patients have with their family members and others. When there is a lack of clear information that results in confusion, distress, and false information, it affects the whole group in negative ways and may jeopardize the patient's medical care and health. When everybody has accurate information, they can communicate about it better and deal with it collectively and more appropriately.

Trains them for self-care procedures – Many patients can benefit by learning how to perform specific self-care procedures to increase their independence, and to reduce their dependence on you and on medical centers. Instruction, demonstration, and practice can enable them to perform these procedures well.

May reduce medical costs – When patients are empowered to play a significant role in their own care, they may be able to reduce costs by making fewer visits to you. Patients who are not educated tend to be more helpless and too dependent on health care providers. When they have knowledge, they know what to expect during their process of care, so they are less likely to make unnecessary visits for unfounded concerns. Also, the more procedures they have been trained to provide for themselves, the lower their medical expenses.

Provides basis for good navigation – Patients get stressed when they don't know how to navigate around medical centers, campuses, or through the process of their care. So teaching them to navigate the facilities and the care process is a great benefit for patients, and they appreciate this practical information as much as the direct health information.

Creates awareness of specific support – Many medical centers and communities offer a range of supportive services for patients such as counselling, social services, and spiritual care. By creating awareness of these services, patients are encouraged to access them when needed. Without clear information about what can help them, many patients don't realize that they have access to these services and how they can benefit by using them.

Motivates further learning – When education programs and materials are well-developed, promoted, and presented, patients see that they have good opportunities to learn reliable information, so they are more likely to choose to learn. Ideally, they see that they have options to learn in more than one way and options to gain detailed information about specific topics. Patients have more motivation, better focus, and better understanding when they have choices of topics and ways to learn.

Provides opportunities for interaction – Patients can learn a lot when they have the chance to interact with health care providers and with other patients. They gain understanding when they can have open discussions during consultations. Group classes and patient conferences give patients the chance to ask questions and get clarification from educators, as well as learn from the questions and comments of other patients with similar health challenges. Learning from peers can often be effective, and may connect patients with each other for emotional support as well.

Can lead to better outcomes – Providing effective patient education is a powerful way to enhance health care to the point where it provides better outcomes. Here is a summary of some of the points presented above that demonstrate how education can produce results for your patients:
- Gets their minds and bodies working in sync for healing.
- Empowers them to actively and effectively participate in their care.
- Defines their roles and increases adherence, self-care, and lifestyle changes.
- Enables them to be proactive so they can better navigate their care and access needed interventions and helpful support.
- May lower stress to benefit their overall wellbeing.
- Increases trust in you so they partner with you more closely.
- Saves them from some of the negative consequences of confusion, false information, misunderstanding, and misdirection.

How Educating Patients Can Benefit Medical Centers

Creates efficiencies – Since informed patients are empowered, they require less time and attention from health care providers. They know how to navigate their care, how to provide self-care, and what types of issues they need interventions for and which ones they don't. Uninformed patients tend to cause more stain on medical centers because they are more confused, helpless, and dependent. So, when you develop education initiatives, design them to create efficiencies.

Saves costs – When education creates efficiencies, medical centers have the chance to reduce expenses. An often-referenced study from the past found that "on average, for every dollar invested in patient education, three to four dollars were saved." It further concluded that if patient education remained stable over time, the return on investment increased, but if patient education stopped, the benefits ceased.[1]

Allows increased focus on core care – Since educated patients are less dependent, they allow health care providers to focus more

---

[1] Bartlett , E.E. (1995). Cost benefit analysis of patient education. *Patient Education Counsel*, 26 (1-3), 87-91.

on essential core issues. Educating patients can help reduce some of the following:

- Unfounded concerns and fears
- Unnecessary visits
- Repetitious explanations and discussions
- Navigation confusion
- Addressing complications caused from ignorance, false information, or non-compliance
- Performance of minor procedures that patients can learn to do themselves

Encourages helpful partnerships with supportive organizations – You can benefit yourselves and your patients by collaborating with other organizations to help educate your patients. Many organizations are very willing and able to contribute to learning options. They have already developed high quality programs and materials. Connecting with these organizations and using their extensive resources can save you from doing everything yourself. Since many of these organizations have charitable funding, they are usually able to provide you with materials and other learning options at no cost since they exist to support the types of patients you see.

Enhances overall care – Planning, developing, implementing, and managing patient education gives health care providers and medical centers a very important dimension of enhanced care. It also gives you another dimension for evaluation and research to continually monitor and improve care and outcomes.

May improve reputation and ratings – Well-educated patients generally feel more valued, nurtured, and empowered, so they are motivated to work in partnership with you for the best results. High satisfaction and improved outcomes can lead to an enhanced reputation and higher ratings for health care providers and medical centers.

Why Educate When There is an Internet?

Since the internet gives patients access to almost limitless sources of health information, you may wonder what's left to teach them. Is it really necessary to educate when many of them already know so much from what they have read, heard, and watched?

The internet actually makes your instruction more essential than if there was no world wide web, because much of the information they get overwhelms, confuses, and misdirects them. The best possibilities for healing will only happen if they are dealing with the real facts about their health challenges and treatments. Since you know their problems best, you and your team are the ones to direct learning and clarify the understanding of your patients.

Problems with Medical Information on the Internet

For nearly every medical problem, the internet can connect searchers to very reliable and helpful information. However, this good information is mixed with many other types of information and misinformation, so patients often have no idea what to focus on or what to believe. Here are some of the characteristics of medical information from websites:

- **Overwhelming amount** – When patients search a health topic, they are barraged with thousands and even millions of website choices. Typing the word *cancer* into Google ® brings up over

500 million choices. Most patients really have no idea where to start and what to trust, so they easily get lost and confused without finding what they seek. If they have not been given search help or guidelines, they are at the mercy of their random selections.

- **Much is written by writers who are not medical professionals** – Every website needs content, and most medical professionals are busy treating patients, so they don't have the time or interest in writing content for the internet. As a result, much of the health information on the web is written by people who are not medically educated or trained. This approach may work well if the content is well vetted through the right professionals, but this vetting is often done superficially or not at all. As a result, much of the content on some sites is confusing and inaccurate.
- **Much has bias** – Since most websites are developed to promote a certain agenda, most of them are not fully objective. The health information they present is written to convince people to think, feel or act in certain ways. Medical sites are often unreliable sources of information because they are developed by:
  o Doctors to promote their services
  o Medical centers to recruit patients
  o Drug companies to promote their products
  o Alternative therapists trying to distract patients from conventional medicine and convince them to try other types of treatments and procedures
  o People and organizations with an agenda to discredit conventional medical care
- **Much does not reflect your practice** – Even if a website is well-developed and reliable, it may not reflect your practice in your medical center. Patients can find many guidelines for treating health problems on the internet, but even so-called evidence-based guidelines tend to vary greatly from one source to another. Guidelines are in constant flux, and treatments available in one country or center may not be available in other places. Some patients will print off guidelines and bring them to you expecting you to follow them when you have very good reasons to treat them in a different way.

- **Much is hard to understand** – Most of the content on most health websites is not written in clear, plain language, so it is not easy for patients to understand. Much of the content is written with concepts and terms that only the medically educated can understand. Patients may be overwhelmed by the complex information and distressed that they can't understand it.
- **Much is inaccurate and outdated** – If health-related websites are not updated regularly, their information is soon outdated. For one reason or another, some sites were created years ago and then neglected or left abandoned. These sites still appear in the searches with information long obsolete. In addition, many sites present inaccurate information either as a part of their biased agenda or because of poor content development.
- **Much undermines you** – The internet is full of sites that undermine conventional health care. They claim that doctors and drug companies are holding back cures so they can make more money from patients. They reject real scientific studies and quote false or unreliable "studies" and stories to make unproven claims. Some sites feature people chatting and posting horror stories of certain types of care by certain doctors at certain centers. While there are reasons to question or complain about some cases of health care, these sites can seriously affect how much patients trust you and the treatments that you offer to help them.

Take the Lead in Helping Patients Learn

If you don't take the lead in helping your patients to learn, then the internet searches by them and their families will most likely take the lead. You have the opportunity to clarify the core information and to give them a framework for further learning. Here are some of the things that you can offer them to counteract internet confusion, misinformation, and misdirection:

- **Advocate evidence-based information and care** – Patients need to know what makes information and health care reliable, so let them know that objective scientific evidence is the most reliable. Let them know how medical studies are set up to ensure objectivity and accuracy. Explain how you are treating

27

them with an evidence-based approach, and that everything they learn about their condition and treatments should be based on reliable evidence.

- **Direct them to reliable sources of information** – After you have explained the core information to them, let them know how to find further information in materials or learning options at the medical center and within reliable websites.
- **Speak with authority** – Your voice needs to come across as more trustworthy than the voices on the internet, so speak clearly and confidently as you address patients and their health issues. In your approach and explanations, give them reasons to trust you.
- **Clarify the core information** – Patients need to know the names of their medical problems, they need to understand the nature of their problems, and they need to understand their treatment options and how they work. Once they have this core information clear, they are less likely to get lost in confusing information outside of this context.
- **Speak as personal partner in their care** – Many websites try to get patients to trust them and partner with what they offer. You need to help them trust you and your medical center as more understanding, more personal, and a more caring partner than anything they see on the internet.

Checklist for Website Selections

The health information on your website, and the other sites to which you direct patients, should have the following characteristics:

☐ Be accurate

☐ Be current

☐ Be based on objective and reliable evidence

☐ Be identified as coming from a reliable institution or other source

☐ Be well-illustrated with high quality visuals

☐ Be reasonably easy to navigate

Ideally, the websites will also have several of the following characteristics, but these are not always essential for the sites to be helpful:

☐ Be easy to understand

☐ Be reflective of the health care that you offer or advocate

☐ Be well-designed

☐ Be objective and mostly unbiased

☐ Be interactive in helpful ways

☐ Be illustrated with animations and other active visuals

☐ Offer interesting and relevant video selections

☐ Have more than one language option for core information

☐ Show real life perspectives and experiences

☐ Offer practical information

☐ Offer formats that print well

☐ Work well on mobile devices as well as computers

☐ Show specific references to the sources of key information provided

☐ Offer links to other good sources of information

Core Approaches and Strategies for Educating Well

How Do Patients Learn Best?

Principles of Adult Education

Teaching adults is different than teaching children. Since children don't have much life experience, they study because they are required to go to school, and they tend not to realize the practical benefits of learning. But adults have years of real life experience beyond their education, so they know the benefits of knowing information that applies directly to their lives. Most adults are keen learners if they see the practical applications of learning, and if they are taught within the context of their life experiences.

Here are some of the principles of adult learning:
Most adults –

- See learning as a means to an end, rather than an end in itself. They need to know what to do and to see progress and results.
- Want learning that is based on real life situations and tasks with a strong "how to" focus.
- Want to actively participate in learning.
- Want to share their own experiences and have them valued.
- Want learning to be immediately useful.
- Want to be treated as equals and to learn cooperatively with their instructors.
- Do not like to appear ignorant or foolish. They will accept challenges or risks once they have some confidence of success.
- Need to know why they should learn, what they will learn, and how the learning will take place.[2]

---

[2] Brandage, D.M. (1980) *Adult learning principles and their application to proper planning.* Ontario Ministry of Education.

Understand Your Patients Better

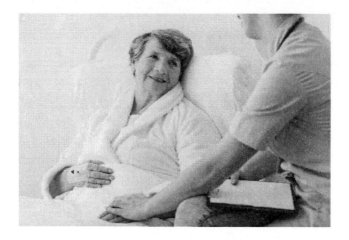

In order to educate your patients, you need to be able to connect with them, understand them, and interact with them. Otherwise your efforts to empower them with knowledge may miss the mark. While there are some similarities in patients, there are also many differences. You may not be able to personalize all learning options, but understanding the things they have in common and the scope of differences will help direct your efforts.

Similarities in Patients

- Like all people, your patients consist of several human dimensions, each affected by health issues. Healing happens best when all dimensions work in sync together:
  - Physical
  - Mental
  - Emotional
  - Spiritual
- Patients are people who have lived through the flow and challenges of their lives so far and have thereby gained valuable knowledge and experience. The experiences of living provide a foundation for further learning. But negative experiences and misconceptions can bias them and hinder further learning.
- Patients want –
  - To be treated kindly and gently
  - To be treated with respect, with a recognition of their human dignity

- o To receive personal attention
- o To understand and to be understood during interactions with their health care providers
- o To receive high quality care with the most effective resolutions to their health problems
- o To be empowered with real choices
- o To feel safe and secure
- o To avoid pain
- o To receive empathy and compassion, when indicated by their care situation
- o To have minimal disruption from the flow and connections of their lives
- o To be as independent as possible
- Patients don't want –
  - o Pain
  - o Uncomfortable tests, procedures, and treatments
  - o To wait for a clear diagnosis of their health problems
  - o To wait for urgent surgeries and treatments
  - o Expenses they can't afford
  - o Difficulty and confusion navigating their care
  - o Difficulty connecting with their health care providers when they have needs or concerns
  - o To be or feel incapacitated and dependant on others
  - o To feel abandoned by their health care providers
- They generally want to understand –
  - o Their health problems and solutions
  - o The best treatment options available to them
  - o Their role and the role of their health care providers
  - o How to navigate their care proactively
  - o How to get help and support for their specific needs
  - o How to feel good and live well during and after their care

Differences in Patients

- The desires to learn and methods of coping vary with patients. Most fall somewhere in between the two following approaches, and all types need help to learn and respond in beneficial ways:
  - o **Monitors** – People who want to learn everything about their condition or risks, and they want to assertively participate in

their care. But monitors can tend to be extra sensitive and over reactive since they are so involved. They may miss some of the main messages by focusing too much on certain details about possible threats.

- o **Blunters** – People who are not very motivated to learn beyond basic information about their condition or risks. They tend not to search out detailed information and don't have much interest in participating in their care. Blunters tend to ignore and deny important information about their health.

- There is no formula indicating how to best educate those who tend to be strong *monitors* or *blunters*. If you are dealing with patients individually, do your best to perceive their approach and direct your teaching accordingly.
  - o Monitors need to be directed to reliable sources of information for further learning, and they need help to understand the information in perspective so they don't get hung up on what they may perceive as overwhelming threats.
  - o Blunters can't be forced to learn and participate since there are usually barriers that cause them to be disinterested. When possible, present them with essential personal health information that connects with their lives in a practical way. Help them to realize how their participation can benefit them in real ways, and then let them know exactly what you recommend them to do.[3]

- Each of your patients consists of a unique combination of such characteristics as –
  - o Age and life experience
  - o Genetics, race, skin color, culture, and sexual identity
  - o Levels of education
  - o Learning approaches and preferences
  - o Learning abilities and disabilities
  - o Medical knowledge
  - o Medical issues, treatments, and prognosis
  - o Personal interests

---

[3] Miller, S.M. & Mangan, C.E. (1983). Interesting effects of information and coping style in adapting to gynaecological stress: Should a doctor tell all? *Journal of Personality and Social Psychology*, 45, 223-236.

- o Attitudes and biases
- o Mental, emotional, and spiritual health
- o Religious beliefs and practices
- o Expectations
- o Past experiences, feelings, and trust with health care
- o Levels of connection and support from families, partners and friends
- o Issues such as dependency, addictions, mental, emotional, spiritual and social challenges
- o Financial resources
- They have various ways of reacting to and dealing with –
  - o Health problems
  - o Medical procedures and treatments
  - o Changes and life disruptions
  - o Providing necessary self-care
  - o Making recommended lifestyle changes
  - o Loss of abilities, function, and control
  - o A poor prognosis and death

Understanding the many similarities and differences of your patients provides a foundation for developing ways to educate them effectively. Here are some ways to use this understanding to connect with patients better:

- When you develop educational programs, materials, and other options, keep the common characteristics of patients primarily in mind, and be as inclusive and sensitive as possible to their differences.
- Use an understanding of these patient characteristics to produce better ways for them to learn so they resonate with patients. They will connect much better with education that addresses their humanity rather than impersonal medical facts or instructions.
- When you have the opportunity to consult directly with individual patients, chat with them to gain an understanding of their personal characteristics, especially if you will be caring for them over a period of time. List some key discussion points as notes to guide you in getting to know them. The better you understand your patients, the better you will connect with them and be able

to encourage them to partner with you for their care.
- Some characteristics can be barriers to learning, so find ways to address them through discussion and education when they appear:
  o Negative past experiences with health care
  o A general disinterest in learning or knowing about their health
  o False information and misconceptions
  o Unrealistic expectations
  o Stress and fears – some emotional issues can be resolved by providing cognitive clarity, but others will need to be addressed by appropriate professionals.

Be Very Clear – Plain Language Guidelines

Speak and write in a clear and simple way so your patients can understand you. No matter how scientific, brilliant, or eloquent your words may be, if patients don't understand, your attempt at educating them will fail.

Studies show that people generally read at a lower level than their level of education would indicate. Even those who are highly educated tend to appreciate health care information that is clear and basic. In addition, patients who primarily use other languages often have a low level of comprehension of your common language, so simplifying your communication will increase their understanding.

Here are some guidelines to help ensure that most of your patients will understand you. At the end of this section, you will find a **Quick Checklist** of these guidelines for easy reference.

Know your objectives – Before you speak or write for patients, make sure you know your objectives. What are the points you really want them to understand? Consider making a brief outline of your main points to guide you. When you know for sure what you want to say, you can then prepare your messages to directly deliver the content.

Understand their personal perspectives – Do your best to put yourself in the place of your patients so you understand their experiences and points of view. Each type of patient has things in common with other similar patients, but also some unique characteristics. Some of them understand medical concepts already, but many do not, so don't assume they know anything for sure. The better you can relate to their personal perspectives, the better you will be able to direct your messages to them. All patients want to be treated as intelligent human beings with a right to know. They also want to be treated with dignity and respect, and they tend to respect you more when you treat them that way.

Use simple, common language – The language of health care professionals is not the language that most patients understand. Use simple and clear words to make your points. Speak conversationally, and use contractions as you do in casual discussions.

Keep the reading level easy – Since many patients have difficulty understanding what they read, make sure to write at a level that most will understand. Some medical educators recommend writing at a Grade 6 reading level to ensure the best comprehension. A more manageable goal is to write at a **Grade 8 reading level** since using necessary medical terms increases the level.

Reading level is generally determined by the number of syllables in words, with more syllables indicating more complexity. A Grade 8 reading level indicates that each sentence contains only one word with 3 or more syllables, on average, so use mostly 1 and 2 syllable words. If you are using Microsoft Word ® you can go into the Review options and select an analysis of the reading level of your writing. But the grade is not the only factor that matters since your writing should also flow clearly from concept to concept.

Be concise – When writing educational materials, make sure to include all essential points but don't use more words or explanations than necessary. The more patients read, the less likely they are to remember the core content. Concise writing is usually clearer because it leaves out unnecessary words and content. When you are consulting with patients, also be as clear and direct as possible.

Use mostly short sentences – Long sentences can cause patients to get confused, so generally speak and write in short sentences of about 10 to 15 words. But make sure the sentences and concepts flow well and sound natural since choppy writing is distracting.

Use mostly short paragraphs – Organize most of your writing into short paragraphs of around 4 or 5 sentences each. But use your discretion and vary the length to some degree so there seems to be a natural flow to the information. The purpose of most paragraphs is to state a main point and support it before going onto your next point in the following paragraph.

Define key words – When you must use medical terms to identify body parts, diseases, conditions, and treatments, define the words when you first use them. If there is a common word for a medical term, let them know the medical term also, but use the common word in most conversations and text. In printed materials, either bold or italicize new words when you first introduce them so they stand out as you define them.

Organize material in sections – When developing printed materials, divide the content into short sections and use headings and subheadings to introduce each section and subsection. This organization will make it easy for patients to read and remember the main points, and easier to find the information they need. Make your headings and subheadings as clear and compelling as possible to create interest and encourage reading. Patients will more likely read sections if the heading appeals to their practical needs or interests.

Writing headings and subheadings as questions sometimes works well when you ask the questions in the headings and then answer them in the material beneath. Be consistent in your approach so the headings work together and so they help the information in the document to flow from one point to the next.

Use bullets – When you are writing a list of similar points, use bullets to make them easy to read and to show that they are similar points. Indent bullets slightly to distinguish them from the regular text. This variation can also add some variety to the page layout. Generally avoid using sub-bullets under main bullets since the layers of bullets can get confusing, but there are places where this option may work well.

Choose the most personal perspective – Speak and write as personably and as directly as possible to patients, and sound conversational rather than distant.

There are **3 perspectives** for speaking and writing:
- **1st person perspective** – when you refer to yourself and your team in a personal way with the pronouns *I, me, my, mine, we, us, our,* and *ours.*
- **2nd person perspective** – when you refer to your patients and family members in a personal way with the pronouns *you, your,* and *yours.*
- **3rd person perspective** – when you want to speak or write from an objective viewpoint and don't refer to yourself or your patients in a personal way. With this approach you refer to patients with general nouns such as *men, women, children, people,* or *patients,* and pronouns *he, him, his, she, her, hers, they, them,* and *theirs.* Refer to health care providers as *doctors, specialists, researchers, nurses, therapists* or whatever name is appropriate.

Here are some guidelines for using these perspectives when consulting and educating your patients:

- Almost always speak and write for your patients in a personal way by using the 2nd person perspective when you refer to them.
- In speaking, almost always refer to yourself and other health care providers with the personal 1st person perspective. When referring to professionals who are not part of your close team, refer to them in the 3rd person perspective.
- In most of your conversations with patients, use both 1st and 2nd perspectives as you refer to yourself and to them in a personal way.
- When you write content for materials or for websites, usually refer to your patients in the personal 2nd person perspective, and to care professionals in the objective 3rd person perspective. But in writing personal letters or notes, write as you would speak using 1st person for yourself and your team and 2nd person in reference to them.
- Use the 3rd person perspective when it seems most appropriate

to be general and objective rather than personal. For example, when you are writing about research or referring to it, this objective perspective is probably most appropriate.

- When you are using the 3rd person perspective, be gender-neutral unless the material is specifically for males or females. For general explanations, use the plural form of pronouns to keep the content gender-neutral. So, use *they* rather than *he/she* and *them* rather than *him/her*.

Be specific rather than general – When you are giving advice or directives to your patients, be as specific as possible. If you are too general, they may be confused, or they may need to call you for clarification, or they may ignore the message since it seemed too vague.

- For example, instead of telling them to *drink lots of fluids*, tell them to *drink 8 glasses a day of water, juice, or herbal tea*. (This statement is meant as an example of how to be specific and is not meant to be real advice since liquid needs can vary.)

Clarify concepts in helpful ways – Many medical concepts are hard for patients to understand, so use examples, stories, comparisons, and illustrations to help clarify concepts.

Be positive rather than negative – Frame your messages to patients in the most positive way possible to be encouraging, rather than coming across negatively with threats. There are cases where some negative realities may need to be emphasized, but patients tend to respond better to encouragement rather than fear tactics.

- For example, emphasize the great benefits of smoking cessation for them rather than reminding them of the dangers that they already know.

Write actively rather than passively – Writing actively means being as direct as possible by placing the **main character before the main action** (main noun before main verb) in most of your sentences. This is the logical way to write since we generally want to know who the character is before we find out what the character is doing. When you use a passive approach, you put the main action before the main character, so it makes the point more confusing because we find out what happened before we know who did it. There are places where passive voice is the most appropriate when you want to make a point about the action more than the character, but your writing will be generally clearer and more direct when you write actively.

- Instead of saying *The cart was pulled by the horse* (passive), say *The horse pulled the cart* (active).
- Instead of saying *The patient was treated by the doctor* (passive), say *The doctor treated the patient* (active).

Write similar points in a similar way – For the sake of consistency and easy understanding, write and present similar points in similar ways. Doing this is called **parallelism** and it helps keep your material professional, organized, and clear.

- For example, if you start off your first bullet with an active verb, then try to start the whole list of the bullets in that section with active verbs.

Be consistent in style and usage – Write and edit documents with a consistent style flowing through each document. It should not seem like it was cut and pasted together from more than one writer, even though you may actually have more than one writer. Also, use words and terms in a consistent way. Don't confuse patients by going back and forth using different terms for the same thing or by switching the way you use words or terms. Generally use words in the ways they are commonly used in regular conversations.

Spell correctly and follow rules of grammar and punctuation – Make sure that you write and edit according to correct spelling and established rules of grammar and punctuation in your country. If your material is full of mistakes, many patients will notice and will be less likely to trust the information since it seems poorly developed.

Avoid abbreviations – While medical staff tend to use and understand multiple abbreviations, don't use them much with patients. Abbreviations referring to such things as conditions, procedures, and departments tend to be misunderstood or meaningless to patients. If you do use abbreviations in your writing, make sure to clearly define them at first appearance.

Use numerals for numbers – When you are using numbers, use the numeral to represent them rather than writing them out as words. Numerals stand out so they are easier to see, read, and remember. They are also usually shorter than the words for them.

- Standard writing rules may indicate that you write out numbers less than 10, but use numerals for all numbers in health care writing.

Don't copy other documents – Never plagiarize written content from other sources since it is illegal to do so. There may be only a few ways to explain some conditions and treatments, so your material may be similar to some other sources, but it must be unique. If you want to use specific information from other sources, arrange legal permission to do so, or provide references to the original sources. If almost everything you want to explain has already been written in other materials or websites, you may find a way to adopt or adapt these other sources rather than trying to redevelop our own version. See the chapter here called *When to Use Existing Information and When to Develop Your Own.*

Quick Checklist for Writing

Here is checklist for quick reference when you are writing for patients. These guidelines for good writing are explained in detail above. Many of these directives apply to your discussions with patients as well as your writing for them.

☐ Clarify the purpose of your writing and then write to meet the objectives.

☐ Write to connect with the point of view of your patients.

☐ Refer to patients in a personal way using *you, your,* and *yours.*

☐ Write simply and clearly using common, conversational language.

- ☐ Be concise in your explanations and instructions, and make most sentences and paragraphs short.

- ☐ Emphasize and define key words.

- ☐ Avoid abbreviations unless they are very commonly understood or defined.

- ☐ Organize information into sections with headings, subheadings, paragraphs, and bullet points, as appropriate for the content.

- ☐ Use parallelism by writing similar points in similar ways.

- ☐ Be direct and specific in your explanations and instructions, and provide enough detail to support your points.

- ☐ Write your sentences actively rather than passively by putting the main character before the main action (main noun before main verb).

- ☐ Be consistent in your style of writing and in your use of words.

- ☐ Make sure to spell correctly and to use the standard rules of grammar and punctuation.

- ☐ Write numbers as numerals.

- ☐ Write freshly and originally, but when you use other sources, always provide the references for them.

- ☐ Ensure that the whole document flows well together.

Show as Well as Tell –
The Importance of Visual Learning

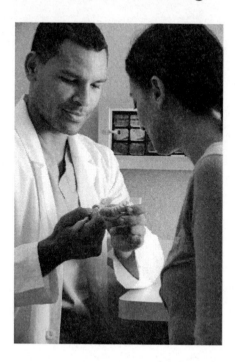

Of all of our senses, our eyes are by far the most significant. Some estimates suggest that about 75% of all that we know, we have learned through our eyes, so keep the importance of visual learning in mind through the development and use of all patient education initiatives. Whether the learning is through consultations, printed materials, presentations, videos, or the internet, strive to show as well as tell. In many cases, a picture really is worth 1000 words or more.

Types of Visual Learning to Implement
- **Photos** – Use photos of almost anything related to health care and healthy lifestyles.
  - Photos should be clear and look professional.
  - Photos should have a main focus without too much clutter to distract from the main focus.
  - Photos work best in color, but black and white can be effective as well.
  - If used in materials, photos should be clearly printed, but

even good quality photocopies are sometimes acceptable.

- **Medical diagrams and charts** – Use diagrams and charts of the body, parts of the body, and medical conditions and diseases.
  - Every consultation room should have printed or electronic medical diagrams or charts available to support consultations.
- **Animated sequences** – Consider using animations of the body to show how the body functions normally and to show the effects of diseases and injuries on the body.
  - You can find these on the internet and in special productions.
- **Illustrations** – Use illustrations of anything related to health care and healthy lifestyles.
  - Keep illustrations simple with strong definition for easy understanding.
- **Simple graphs** – Use graphs to illustrate and clarify important data and medical patterns.
  - Consider using charts and graphs to motivate patients to make progress toward important health goals.
  - Graphs can easily confuse patients so use them sparingly and make them very clear and simple.
- **Maps** – Use to help patients navigate around locations such as medical centers, the medical campuses, and parking locations.
- **Floor plans** – Use to help patients navigate the levels, departments, and services of medical centers.
- **Media slides** – Use to enhance learning during presentations so patients can see as well as hear the information.
  - Try to include visuals on at least half of the slides, and don't overcrowd your slides with text.
  - Use photos, cartoons, graphs, illustrations, embedded videos, and other colorful visuals to support the important points.
  - If they are not developed well or not used in sync with your explanations, media slides can be a distraction rather than a benefit. Develop them to reflect the nature of the presentations.
- **Videos** – Make and use videos to show scope, process, action, and interactions. Videos can bring almost any place, any process, and any relationship into vivid focus.

- o Videos work very well to show virtual tours, patient experiences, self-care instructions, and many other concepts in health care.
- **Website visuals such as icons, photos, illustrations, videos, and animation** – Use many types of visuals to make your website interesting and effective.
  - o Websites will be ignored if they don't have lots of visual support for the words.

Here are some of the ways that visuals can enhance learning:

- **Creates interest** – Visuals usually draw much more attention than words alone.
- **Makes learning easier** – When you use visuals effectively, they help make learning easier. Patients can learn a concept at a glance.
- **Supplements your words** – Verbal and written words will always be a fundamental way to present information to patients, but visuals will bring more attention to the words and help patients understand the explanations.
- **Helps patients remember** – People tend to remember what they see better than what they just hear or read, so visuals alone, or along with words, make a more lasting impression.
- **Adds personal and emotional elements** – Photos and videos can show real people in real life or health care situations. Bringing in these personal and emotional appeals creates interest and can make a big difference in encouraging and inspiring lifestyle changes. Persuasion usually requires affecting both the intellect and the emotions of your patients.

Using visuals makes patient education more diverse and interesting for health care educators as well, and it helps you create better printed materials, better presentations, and better websites. When you think about concepts visually, you can more easily find the focus of your main points and be inspired to make the information clear for patients in new ways. But work to find the right balance of visuals to words in whatever you are writing, developing, or presenting. The balance may vary from project to project, but experience and evaluation will reveal what works best in helping to educate and empower your patients.

Unfortunately, there are many people who are visually handicapped and blind. For them, illustrations offer little or no benefit, although their family members may be helped. So, keep those with disabilities in mind and find ways to help them learn through their ears, through touch, and through experience. Even though your main focus is probably on helping those who can see, also think of meaningful ways to help the visually impaired.

Design Everything Well

Design your pages, your materials, your media slides, and your website well. Your clear writing may be ignored or misunderstood if you don't present it within the context of good design.

Design professionally – Your patients see professionally designed information and promotions everywhere on billboards and websites, and in commercials, newspapers, magazines. So make sure that your creations are well-designed or they may stand out for their poor appearance. There is a place for simple documents that have not been professionally designed, but get experts involved in important productions. When information is presented in a professional way, people tend to trust it more than information that is arranged poorly. Even though you may think something looks good from your perspective, you will probably overlook important elements and principles if you are not trained in design.

Professional designers know how to make attractive designs, but they don't always arrange the information in a simple and clear way. Work with the designers to ensure that all elements will be easy for patients to see and understand. You may want to refer to the *Detailed Checklist for Good Design* presented here.

If you don't have the budget to hire professional graphic and web designers, then at least arrange for them to review your materials and website developments before you finalize them. Consider contacting a local university or art school to arrange for some design students to assist you as volunteers.

Be aware of the elements and principles of design – If you are not a graphic designer yourself, don't get overwhelmed with the many elements and principles of design, because it takes professional training to understand and use them well. However, you should be aware of these factors so you realize their importance and can work along with designers as they employ them in your developments.

Here are the basic **elements** of design. These components create the appearance of all visual creations:
- Lines
- Shapes
- Forms
- Spaces
- Colors
- Textures
- Values
- Typography (styles of printed text)

Here are some of the basic **principles** of using these elements to create attractive illustrations, materials, websites, and media slides:

- **Unity** – Design all elements to work together to create the planned impression.
- **Harmony** – Design all features to complement each other in a positive and attractive way.
- **Hierarchy** – Arrange information and elements according to their importance.
- **Emphasis** – Make key information and elements stand out more than others.
- **Alignment** – Show order and organization that looks good and helps learning.
- **Balance** – Design so that the visual weight of such features as light, dark, text, illustrations, and spaces are distributed well.
- **Proportion** – Decide on how much space each element should take in relation to all other elements.
- **Contrast** – Make sure opposing elements such as light and dark and horizontal and vertical lines work together for visual clarity.
- **Variety** – Create visual interest by using selected variations in the design, while still maintaining unity.
- **Repetition** – Repeat some information and style elements to reinforce their importance and to create a rhythm in your design patterns.
- **Movement** – Design to keep the eyes of readers moving well with the flow of information.

For more information on the elements and principles of design, and for good examples, refer to the vast resources on the internet and multiple books dealing with this topic.

Create templates for materials – If you don't already have professionally designed materials, or if you are changing your designs, create templates to use as the framework for all of the materials you develop. These templates should include the important elements and principles of design and provide the basic style and structure for all of your pages and materials.

- After the templates are developed, you may get professionals to put all of your new information into these templates, or you may choose to format the documents yourself by entering new or updated content into the created templates.

- If you will be printing some of your material in color and others with only black ink, design the templates to work well with both color and without. Color is an important feature of some designs, but make sure the design also works with black ink only. Even when you print some documents with black ink, you can use colored paper to add variety and interest.
- On the cover templates, leave room for a big and bold title. Also leave room for a photo or illustration on most covers to distinguish each document and to create interest.
- Include your logo appropriately on all templates, but don't use the logo as the main design element. The title should stand out more than anything else.
- The pages that follow the cover should feature distinguishing design elements but remain mostly open for the content. You may use one feature from the cover, such as a vertical or horizontal line, as the design feature on the content pages. Don't overuse the logo by placing it on every page of a multi-page document.

Create 3 template sizes – If you work at a large medical center and will be developing various materials, design 3 basic templates to use for all of your materials. If you plan to develop only a few materials, or make everything the same size, then pick one of the following standard sizes:

- **Pamphlet size** – this size is generally equal to a letter-sized sheet of paper folded in 3 panels or a legal-sized sheet folded in 4 panels.
  - o Pamphlets can be created as one big sheet folded into panels, or they can be cut into panels, using staples to hold them together, if you have more than one sheet.
  - o Create designs for front cover, internal pages, and the back page. The back page can be the same as the internal pages, or different if you want to add your logo, contact information, or other features.
- **Booklet size** – generally equal to a letter-sized sheet of paper folded in 2, but can vary with specially cut paper.
  - o Can be used as a 4 panel brochure, or it can contain several

pages stapled together.

- o Can be designed with a front and back cover, or designed without any special covers.
- o Create designs for front cover, internal pages, and the back cover. The back page can be the same as the internal pages, or different if you want to add your logo, contact information, or other features there.
- **Full page size** – generally equal to an unfolded letter-sized sheet of paper.
  - o Can be used as one-sided or two-sided handout, or it can be a full-sized booklet with several pages attached.
  - o Create designs for each type of page you choose to use. The first page can be a cover, a title page, or a heading followed by content.
  - o If you are developing these full-sized documents, consider breaking the text into 2 columns on each page since it's easier to read columns than to follow lines all the way across a big page.

If you are creating documents of more than one size, make sure that all of the template sizes work together as a "family" of printed materials. Even though the sizes are different, they should feature the same basic design elements so it is obvious that they all come from your health care center and work together to inform patients.

Detailed Checklist for Good Design

☐ **Use simple, clean, clear design features** – Even though you have a choice of many elements of design, be selective in how you use them since too many design features may distract from the content.

☐ **Make titles and headings big and bold** – Use titles and headings throughout your materials and websites to divide the information into smaller learning sections. Make them bigger and bolder than regular text so the various sections are easy to find and follow.

☐ **Don't clutter pages** – Space is a key element of design, so include appropriate space breaks and free space on each page to balance the content.

☐ **Use color sparingly** – Use some color on your materials for visual enhancement, if your budget allows, but be careful about using too many colors or too much color since this sensory overload will distract from the educational content. A full range of colors is appropriate for some illustrations and photos.

☐ **Use fonts that are easy to read** – Some designers suggest that *serif type font* is the easiest to read since the letters have little tails to help tie them together, but others suggest that *sans serif* (without tails) is just as easy to read. If you are trying to decide which fonts work best with your patients, print off some samples of text in different fonts, side by side, and ask a full spectrum of patients which ones they prefer.

☐ **Use only 2 styles of font** – It is very acceptable to use one style of font for titles and headings and another style for the main text, so choose this approach if you wish. But make sure that both styles work well together. There are situations and documents where more than 2 styles are acceptable, but don't use more than 2 styles unless a professional designer has offered a good reason for doing so. With too many styles, the document can look disjointed and poorly designed.

☐ **Use 12 point font or bigger for main text** – Patients prefer to read text that is at least a 12 point size and many prefer a 13 or 14 point size. Bigger font size is easier to read, so use at least 12 point to help encourage reading and learning. For titles and headings, use larger point sizes than your main text.

☐ **Line up print on the left but not the right** – The left margins should be lined up evenly (justified) but it's best to leave the right side of your text jagged (not justified). Lining up text on the right side leaves less balancing space, makes the text seem more crowded, and it often requires that words get stretched, squashed or spliced to make them fit into this unnatural layout.

☐ **Use non-glare paper for main content** – Shiny paper reflects light more strongly and causes glare. Covers for brochures and booklets can be printed on shiny paper since this helps them stand out at first glance, but use non-glare paper for the main educational content. Some promotional materials work well on glossy paper if there is not too much text.

☐ **Use bold and boxes for emphasis** – Help key words stand out by bolding them or by putting them in italics. It's also effective to emphasize some key content by putting it in a box within the text. Don't overuse bold or boxes or they become distracting and less effective. If you place content within a box, make sure the design helps bring attention to the box since it may be ignored if it seems to be too separate.

☐ **Don't use all caps** – When you print a heading or other text in all capital letters, it becomes more difficult to read because all of the letters appear as blocks of print without variation. To emphasize, use bold, italics, bigger sizes, and boxes. As a general rule, don't use all capital letters for words or titles.

☐ **Support content visually** – Visual support helps patients understand their conditions, treatments, and experiences, and visuals can also help them to remember important concepts better. As appropriate, use photos, diagrams, charts, and graphs to illustrate important concepts.

☐ **Use a *Table of Contents* for long materials** – To make it easy for patients to find and select the content of longer pamphlets and booklets, include a *Table of Contents* near the beginning. Most materials longer than 6 pages should generally have a Table of Contents.

☐ **Code your materials** – Develop and use a simple coding system for all of the educational materials you develop, and print a code on each one. A coding system will help you to manage the materials as you identify, organize, order, distribute, update, and store them. Here are some ideas about codes:

- Keep the code short and simple – less than 20 characters, if possible.
- The code should be a part of each new and updated document and fit somewhere into the design of each one. Printing the code in small print at the bottom of the first or last page works well. Make it small enough so it does not distract from the design and does not confuse patients.
- Things to consider including in the code:
  - Date when the document was originally produced
  - Date of latest revision
  - Department
  - Category of document , such as disease type
  - Printing codes – Identify such things as paper types, color, and number within a series. Greatly abbreviate this type of information.

How to Increase Interest and Learning Retention

We use our senses to learn about the world around us. Generally, the more senses we use in the learning process, the greater the impact and the better our retention. The following figures on remembering should be regarded as general approximations rather than hard data, but they help emphasize the importance of offering full learning experiences.

Adults generally remember about:

- 10% of what we READ
- 20% of what we HEAR
- 30% of what we SEE
- 50% of what we HEAR and SEE
- 70% of what we SAY or DISCUSS with others
- 80% of what we EXPERIENCE personally
- 90% of what we SAY and DO[4]

So, through all of your education initiatives, appeal to as many senses as possible and as reasonable to increase the interest, impact, and retention of your patients. Here are some suggestions for adding sensory dimensions to learning options:

---

[4] Glaser, R. (1983, June). Education and Thinking: The Role of Knowledge. Technical Report No. PDS-6. Pittsburgh, PA: University of Pittsburgh, Learning and Development Center.

- Visually support almost every important concept that you say or write for your patients. These illustrations help them learn by seeing, as well as by hearing and reading. Photos, diagrams, charts, graphs, cartoons, tours, demonstrations, and videos all help the learning process.
- Encourage patient interaction and discussion within most learning situations, including consultations, classes, and presentations. Ask them questions, and give them a chance to pose questions and make comments since these interactions increase their focus, processing, learning, and retention. Discussions help them to think about concepts and experiences and to connect the information to their real lives.
- When some directives need to be especially clear, explain and demonstrate the process, and then ask patients to tell you step by step how they will perform these tasks at home. That way you can be sure they have understood, plus they will remember the instructions better after repeating them in a way that relates to their actual experience.
- When you empower patients with knowledge, give them opportunities to demonstrate what they have learned, when reasonable to do so. Patients are motived to learn both before and during the demonstrations, and they generally remember what they have demonstrated. Here are some ways to get them to show what they have learned:
  o Get them to demonstrate self-care procedures after you have shown them the steps.
  o In some group learning sessions, get patient volunteers to act as characters or props for demonstrations or for simple dramatizations of concepts.
  o When encouraging lifestyle changes, give your patients an easy way to monitor and record the progress of their changes. They can then see how their actions affect their health, demonstrating what you have taught them. Use their created records as points of discussion and further encouragement.

How to Promote Education Programs
to Get Participation

Core education should be integrated into the process of care so all patients receive the most important information that will help them. But also offer special and advanced learning options that are recommended but not required. To get patients and family members to participate in optional learning opportunities, you need to promote them effectively. Promotion yields great results when it is well prepared and directed. Here are some strategies for effective promotion of optional learning programs:

Appeal to their viewpoints and interests – In all types of promotion, appeal to the viewpoints and interests of your patients to get their attention and participation. Consider what they may be thinking and feeling during their care. They may have concerns, they may be confused, they want to be healed, and they want practical information that will help them be healthy. If you connect with where they are at, you can lead them to learning experiences where they can be empowered with knowledge.

Promote at orientation and in patient guide – If most of your patients attend an orientation or receive a patient guide, then use these far reaching sessions and information sources to encourage your patients to learn as much as they can. Emphasize the big role that patients play in their overall care and how learning may help them achieve better health outcomes. List the learning options available to them and strongly encourage them to participate and gain the benefits of knowledge.

Develop schedules, calendars, and brochures – Develop schedules, calendars, and brochures to promote your learning programs and events. Print copies and put them in racks, hand them out, post event calendars on bulletin boards, and feature electronic versions of these promotions on your website.

Be bright, bold and compelling – To catch the attention and interest of patients, develop promotion that stands out. The medical center may already be crowded with bulletin boards, media screens, racks, signs, and posters, and patients tend to tune out the clutter and ignore most of what they see. So, you'll need to find ways to appeal to them:

- Create compelling titles and headings.
  - For example, instead of calling a class *Nutrition for Patients*, you'll get more response from titles such as *Eating for Your Life* or *The Power of Nutrition for You*.
- Use bold print for titles and headings.
- Use bright colors of paper or ink.
- Use appropriate photos, images, and artwork.
- Use good layout design that is attractive, simple, and uncluttered.
- Place promotion in very visible and strategic places.

If you have any influence or control of what is displayed on the walls of your medical center, do whatever you can to keep things clean and uncluttered. Clutter is stressful to patients and staff. Put racks, bulletin boards, signs, and digital screens in key locations, but keep most of the walls clean with only attractive art. Patients will pay more attention to a few key areas of promotion than they will to stuff scattered everywhere. Also keep your bulletin boards and racks organized and neat.

Promote in newsletters – If your medical center has printed or online newsletters, find ways to promote educational programs and events in them. Newsletters generally reach a wide audience and can create awareness and solicit a good response. See more in the chapter entitled *How Newsletters Can Help to Educate*.

Use your website and social media – Your website is a showcase for promoting learning options for patients. Feature a **clear icon** that leads patients to your event schedules and promotions. You may consider an icon with a choice of the following words, or something similar:

- Patient Events for You
- Patient Learning Options

- Help for Patients
- What Patients Need to Know

Your event calendar should be easy to see and understand. Your promotion for programs and events should be short, to the point, and compelling to their interests. Bold headings, colour, photos and images can all help to make your promotion interesting and convincing.

For social media, consider using brief variations of your web features. Your website is core, but you may also find effective ways to get patients connected to your Facebook, Twitter or other social media accounts to keep them updated.

Target handouts – One good way to promote programs and events to patients is through targeted handouts. For certain periods of time, arrange for reception areas, nurses, or other care providers to hand out specific promotional materials to selected types of patients. Determine how to best target these patients during the process of their care. Develop collaborative relationships with those who are going to be involved in the promotion so they realize its importance and are motivated to help. Some groups of patients will already be getting specific materials, so you may be able to add your promotion to something they already receive.

Target mailouts – Targeted mail or email promotion can work very well to get the attention and participation of patients and families. You may work at a small office where you can easily arrange a mailout. Some medical centers will allow you to access patient records and data professionals to organize a mailout to certain types or groups of patients. They can use electronic programs to identify certain types of patients. Most medical centers have large and detailed patient databases that are accessed regularly for research purposes. Since these targeted mailouts reach only the types of patients you select, you have a captive audience for promotion that appeals directly to them. For example, if you work in a cancer center, you can promote a major learning session for colorectal patients by mailing promotion directly to them only. If you decide to organize targeted mailouts, here are some suggestions:

- Use this type of promotion very selectively for major programs or events.

- Make sure you have permission from medical center administration and the privacy commissioner.
- Prepare the mailout list so it includes only appropriate patients from the database, making sure not to include patients who have died or others who may not be appropriate.
- Send a short letter with the promotion to let patients know how their names were selected within the scope of confidentiality and privacy. Also let them know that this learning option is designed to benefit them as a part of their care. Include contact information for you or an associate to address questions or concerns. Patients will be upset if they think their private information has been given to somebody other than their care providers.
- Since the programming of the database will not always be perfect, include a small disclaimer at the bottom of the letter you send with the promotions. You may choose to say something like this: *Based on our current records, we have done our best to send this information to the patients who can benefit most. We sincerely apologize if you received this information inappropriately.*
- Use envelopes that do not have the name of your office or the medical center, especially if the name of the center includes the name of their medical condition. If a patient's name is associated with the name of a medical center on an envelope, some would consider this a breach of privacy. The return address on the envelope can be a specially selected return location that doesn't reveal the identity of the sender.
- Don't send the mailout too early or too late. If you send something too early, patients may forget about the event by the time it occurs. If you send it too late, patients will complain that they didn't have enough notice. Sending it out 3 to 4 weeks before a major event is usually appropriate.

While coordinating mailouts may seem to be a complex hassle at first, once you work out a system for making them happen, they are an excellent way to promote.

Promote on digital information screens – One of the very best ways to catch the attention and interest of your patients is to use digital information screens in strategic locations, such as busy waiting areas. Inserting selected promotion for upcoming events will get a lot of attention on these screens, if the promotion is well developed and clear. Since you can only offer limited information on the screens, at the end of the promotion direct patients to brochures, calendars, or a website for further details.

Make posters – Even though we live in a digital age, posters still have value. Design and print posters and post them in key areas such as elevators and bulletin boards. Posters can be simply created on a computer, or they can be professionally designed. Posters have a limited effect, but they do help create awareness and interest as a supplement to other types of promotion. If you want your posters to have maximum impact, post 3 of them together, vertically or horizontally, in key locations.

Get care providers to promote – Since doctors, nurses and other health care providers consult with patients regularly, they can be very influential in letting patients know about learning programs and sessions. To facilitate this type of promotion, connect with key care providers to make sure they are aware of the education options and understand how these options can benefit their patients. Give promotional brochures or cards to these professionals to hand to their patients.

Make the most of word of mouth – Word of mouth has long been one of the most effective agent of promotion, so it can also work well to promote patient learning options This promotion will happen naturally if all of your learning sessions are well prepared and presented to meet the real needs of patients. By consistently empowering patients with interesting and practical information, the ones who have benefitted from participation will spontaneously recommend the programs and sessions to other patients.

Put up signs on event days – On event days, solicit attention by posting event signs at strategic locations. Place signboards near the medical center entrance and at the doors to the events. If you have digital information screens, program them to flash information about the events in the hours before they begin. All of this promotion creates awareness and encourages attendance for current and future sessions. For the sake of drop-ins on event days, make sure the signs indicate that all are welcome, if the event is not full.

Offer learning rewards – People like to receive recognition and rewards for their accomplishments, so think of ways to reward your patients for choosing to participate in learning options. For example, you may set up "certificates of achievement" for certain types of patients to encourage them to participate in several programs. Give them a checklist of learning options that can benefit them. Then let them know that by participating in a certain number of options and checking them off, they will receive a special certificate of learning, like a "health passport." For instance, if they attend optional classes on nutrition, exercise and sleeping well, then they can receive a "lifestyle improvement certificate" to reward their accomplishment. There are many other ways to reward learning as well.

Only consider offering these learning rewards if you have enough learning options, time, and resources to coordinate it. Plan well and professionally, and then follow through with what you promise. If you are preparing certificates or health passports for them, make sure that they are well designed and look good with their names spelled correctly on them. You may consider offering helpful gifts instead of certificates for some learning accomplishments. Plastic folders, carry bags, or water bottles with the medical center logo on them may be appropriate, if you have the funding.

How to Get Patients to Participate in Their Care

You want your efforts to educate patients to have an impact. You want them to learn, to actively participate in their care, and to make lifestyle changes for the sake of their health. Some keen patients are self-motivated to learn and to do everything they can for the sake of their health. Other patients need you to motivate them. This job of educating patients is not easy, and getting patients to change is not an exact science, but with commitment and strategy, you can make a remarkable difference in the well-being of your patients.

Here are some of the ways that you may want to help your patients get involved and make changes:

- Come for their health care appointments
- Get and take prescribed medications
- Consent to beneficial treatments
- Closely follow instructions for surgery and treatment preparation and recovery
- Provide competent self-care
- Become more independent so they depend less on care providers
- Get needed therapy or counselling
- Participate in learning options so they become empowered with helpful knowledge
- Monitor and record their health data at home
- Find ways to cope well and live well
- Eat better
- Lose weight

- Exercise
- Reduce or stop drinking
- Stop smoking

Strategies to Enable Active Participation and Change

Depending on your role as a health care provider, you see and affect patients at various times and ways. Some of you have direct contact with patients over an extended period of time and therefore can influence them in a big way. But even if you play only a small part in their care, you may be able to make a powerful impression. You won't be able to apply all the following strategies to all of your patients, but keep them in mind and apply them whenever you can to enable patients to participate in their care and to make important lifestyle changes:

Clarify the facts – Always let patients know exactly what is happening with them, especially when you want them to get involved in helping to manage or resolve their problems. Presenting the facts about their health problems and solutions provides the foundation for participation and change. Show them the direct link between their role and its effect on their health.

In situations where they may have caused their critical health conditions, let them know the seriousness of their problems and their essential role in helping to deal with them. If there are real threats to their health, clearly emphasize these threats and let them know how to reduce them. Generally emphasize the positive over the negative, but some patients won't try to change until the danger of the threats has been made very clear to them. Threats and fears can sometimes be a catalyst for change.

Give them specific instructions – When you need patients to participate in their care give them specific and clear instructions about their role, both verbally and in written form. Compliance is much better when the directives leave no room for confusion.

Emphasize the benefits – Let patients know the potential benefits of their participation. Be as specific as possible to make these benefits more understandable and desirable. Patients may have a vague idea of what they should do or how they should live, but they often don't understand the science behind it all. Explain how their actions, their adherence, and their lifestyle changes can create real benefits. To move forward, they need a vision of where this journey can lead.

Help remove barriers – When barriers seem to be getting in the way of patient involvement, do what you can to help remove them. If the barriers are imagined, help the patients to see their situations more objectively so they realize these issues are not real barriers. If the barriers are real, provide support for overcoming them, if possible. For example, if they lack supplies for self-care, help them to access the supplies. If addictions are the barrier, connect them with local support groups or rehab. If their home environment is negative, connect them with social workers who may be able to transition them to a better environment.

There are some barriers that cannot be removed, and some issues require much more attention than you can offer, but you can achieve much by making efforts to understand, support, and direct these patients, both as individuals and as groups.

Get families involved – Family members generally want patients to be well, so they are motivated to get involved in the process of care. When possible, discuss the helpful roles of patients and family members in dealing with the current health issues. These family members can provide some of the care directly, and they can also enable and monitor patients in providing their own care and making changes. If family members are positive, encouraging, and practical, their impact will be most effective.

Teach them self-care skills – When you want patients to perform self-care procedures, train them well, and then give them a chance to demonstrate their skills and ask questions. If patients feel competent and confident, they will much more likely choose to provide their own care in these specific ways. You can train them as individuals or groups, depending on the nature of the procedures.

Empower them – Patients' beliefs about their abilities, as well as their actual abilities, are big factors in determining participation, adherence, and change. Many patients can learn to recognize and use their abilities, and they can then be supported to maximize their efforts. Let patients know that they really have the power to influence their health and outcomes. Some patients have become too dependent on health care providers and need to be convinced that they can play an important role and be more independent. If you want patients to get involved, make it clear that you are empowering them to do so. Help them to see how their choices lead to self-actualization and better health. Also make sure to provide them with the information, training, supplies, or whatever resources they need to be empowered.

Offer them perspective – Offer patients perspective so they can see themselves in a context that rewards participation and change.

- If their views are too narrow, help them to see their lives in a broader scope. Perceptions are what patients think about themselves, others, or external factors. If the perceptions don't reflect the real situations, do what you can to enlighten them so they are able to see and deal with reality.
- If they see their health issues in isolation, help them to see how their mental, emotional, and spiritual natures are all connected with their physical wellbeing, and how all of their dimensions work best together.
- If they have distracting ideas or feelings that get in the way of change, show them how these thoughts and emotions are not based on evidence. For example, if some harmful lifestyle choices have been promoted as positive, help them to see the sobering reality. If they are worried about what other people want or think, help them to realize that these people may be poor influences that should be exchanged for more positive relationships, if possible.
- If they have had bad experiences in the past, empathize with them, but also help them to realize that those experiences don't need to determine the future.
- If they feel that their participation won't make a difference, let them know what power they have and what they can do to gain even small benefits. Show them evidence and examples of how their choices can directly affect their health.

Treat their depression – Ask or screen patients to find out if they are depressed. If they are, treat them or direct them to other professionals for effective treatment. When patients are depressed, they are much less willing and able to participate in their health care. Depression is a serious issue that needs to be addressed or it may hinder all other efforts to get them involved.

Motivate and affirm them – Your patients should be motivated to participate for the possibility of improved outcomes and better health, so make sure they understand this reward. Strengthen their intentions, and motivate them in supportive ways as well. When they do participate, acknowledge what they are doing with a smile and words of encouragement to keep doing it. Verbal affirmation can be powerful.

When you want patients to make lifestyle changes, give them an easy way to record and keep track of any progress they make. Develop a simple card or form where they can record data or check off boxes. Anything they record is a visual sign of progress which helps them feel good about what they have done so far. Ask them to show you their record of progress at each consultation so you can add your verbal affirmation. If their health improves over a period of time, associate this improvement with their choice to participate in their care. Most people don't get much affirmation, so they will appreciate and look forward to receiving it from you, when appropriate.

Reach their hearts – Offer emotional appeals to patients, as well as intellectual, since people generally need to be affected in both ways to make lifestyle changes. Help patients to realize that their health issues are a factor in keeping or losing the things they love most about life. When they realize that their participation may affect their ability to participate in life, they are more likely to want to do what they can. As mentioned earlier, fears can sometimes work as a catalyst, if framed appropriately.

You may hesitate dealing with the emotions of your patients, but you don't need to get deep or complex. For example, you may simply ask patients a few questions about their families, vacations, plans, or interests to get them to focus on these things. Then when you are recommending that they do something specific, you can mention that they seem to have a lot to live for, and encourage them to partner with you in their care.

Inspire them – Sometimes, just an extra bit of inspiration is what patients need to get involved as a partner with you in their health care. Inspiration generally involves getting them to consider and connect with the meaning of their lives, beyond the medical center setting. Photos, videos, quotations, and stories can all help to inspire patients. It may be difficult to offer much inspiration during consultations, so try offering it more peripherally with posters, displays, videos, and website features. Group learning sessions such as classes and patient conferences are excellent opportunities to inspire patients with featured presenters, patient testimonies, panel discussions, video features, and interviews.

Get Patients to Develop a Plan for Change

When you want patients to make lasting lifestyle changes for the sake of their health, get them to develop a plan that will work best for them. Let them know the specific changes and goals that you strongly recommend, but let them decide how to implement these changes in their lives. If they have the chance to be involved in the planning, they will likely come up with a more workable plan than an impersonal one imposed upon them.

Here is the framework for a plan that may be helpful for your patients. Consider preparing a short guiding document such as a worksheet with spaces for responses. Include the following sections, modified and directed to their situation:

☐ **Goals** – List the specific lifestyle changes and goals that have been recommended by your health care provider.

☐ **Reasons** – List the reasons for making important lifestyle changes.

☐ **Benefits** – List the health benefits that you may experience from making these changes.

☐ **Timeline** – Create a timeline showing:
- What changes you will make
- How you will make them
- When you will make them.

For some hard changes, you may need to plan for small, manageable steps over weeks or months. Look at change as a process rather than a sudden leap. Plan how to make these changes permanent.

☐ **Milestones and rewards** – Within the timeline, set milestones that demonstrate times of success, and think of what rewards to give yourself for each accomplishment.

If you have specific health goals such as losing weight, lowering blood pressure, or stopping smoking, link the milestones to progress indicators

☐ **Challenges** – List the main challenges (barriers) that may get in the way of making these changes, and briefly explain how you will work to overcome each of these challenges.

☐ **Support** – List your main sources of support for making these changes, and include connection information for each. If you believe in a Higher Power, include this Power as part of your support.

☐ **Belief** – Make a positive statement about yourself and your goals showing that you are motivated, that you believe in yourself, and that you will move forward confidently. Keep repeating this statement as you make decisions for progress, day after day.

Discuss their plans with them after they have outlined them. Patients feel empowered when they are encouraged to actively plan for making changes, and the planning process gets them involved right away.

How to Use Stories to Educate Patients

Our lives are a series of chapters in a continuous story. Each chapter includes a narrative of our growth, our challenges, our interactions, our feelings, and our achievements. When we think back on our lives, it is our unique and special stories that stand out most. The knowledge we recall best is what we learned in story form, as it related to real life, real insight, and real progress. And when we think of the future, we create a story of how we want our lives to unfold according to our desires, our goals, and our dreams.

A **story** (or narrative) is the account of events or incidents of anyone or anything. Stories can be spoken, written, or shown through various types of photos, art, video, and film. Good stories are able to capture and hold our attention, and they are able to take our minds and emotions into other worlds and other characters. When we realize that we are active agents affecting our own stories, we are all the more engaged because we want them to progress well.

Patients who are dealing with medical issues are in the midst of dealing with unwanted drama. For many, this narrative is filled with stress and fears, new experiences, new relationships, and a desire for a positive outcome. It may be a minor story of getting a few stitches for a cut, or it may be a major one where they fight aggressive cancer along with their medical team. It may be a long story of chronic conditions, of rehabilitation and recovery, or it may be a short tragedy where the frantic efforts of the emergency doctors are not enough to save them.

Since life is a story, effective education works best within a narrative structure. In whatever way is reasonable and possible, educate your patients within the framework of stories that relate to their lives. Don't separate education out of their reality. They will be much more engaged if they realize that they can learn to play a role that affects the outcome of their current health challenges.

The Parts of a Story

You have probably all read stories, studied stories, told stories, and written stories. To remind you, here are the components of stories. But you don't need to think about all of these things when you are listening to patients' stories or using stories to help them learn. Stores can be anything you want them to be, but this reminder might help you hear them and tell them a little bit better.

- **Characters** – the people and other active beings, creatures, and animated forces who are involved in the story
  o There is generally a main character and surrounding characters
- **Point of view** – the perspective from which the story is told Either from the view of one of the characters or an objective viewpoint
- **Setting** – the locations where the story takes place
- **Plot** – the flow of the story
- **Conflict** – the main issue that the characters face and try to resolve The main types of human conflict are:
  o Humans in conflict with other humans
  o Humans in conflict with nature
  o Humans in conflict with themselves
- **Climax** – the most intense part of the conflict
- **Resolution** – how the conflict is resolved
  o May be triumph or defeat, anywhere in between, both, or left somewhat unresolved (just like in real life)

Stories generally progress in the following way, but let them flow in whatever way seems most natural in your patient interactions.

Introduction ▶ Rising action ▶ Climax ▶ Falling action ▶ Resolution

There are some obvious implications here. In the setting of a medical center, the patients are the main characters, and health care providers are the supporting characters. The injuries and diseases are the main sources of conflict, and the plots are the progression of interactions and interventions leading to the best possible outcomes. But, since most real life stories are complex, there can be many other characters and viewpoints, more than one type of conflict, many dramatic climaxes, and a mixture of resolutions.

How Stories Can Help Patients Learn

Clarify meaning – Stories can help to clarify the meaning of many concepts and experiences in health care in the following ways:
- They can present complex medical information in a simple way.
- They have a flow that ties points together in a progressive order.
- They can show how treating injuries and diseases is a narrative with various interventions and outcomes.
- They can connect medical care to real life experiences.
- They help patients see themselves as real characters in their medical dramas, and this objective realization can inspire them to play an active and effective role.
- When patients hear the stories of other patients dealing with their health challenges, they learn how their attitude and approach can impact how well they cope and survive.

Patients tend to make up stories about their health, if they lack understanding. Since these false stories do not reflect their real situations, they can disempower patients from effectively participating in their care. Help them to find meaning by offering clear information to support their reality.

Offer emotional impact – Stories can affect our emotions, as well as our intellect. Stories compel us to relate and react, to laugh or cry, and to change our viewpoints and our behaviours. Stories can inspire and lift our spirits. Since stories can affect patients emotionally, they may add more impact than didactic teaching alone.

74

Create interest – Stories are more interesting than direct medical information so they catch and hold the attention of patients. Increased interest results in better focus and thereby better learning.

Help memory – Since stories have a progressive flow, and since they create interest and engage patients on various levels, patients remember them better than just facts, explanations, and instructions. What you teach within the context of stories, may be easily recalled anytime they reflect on the stories.

Inspire change – Patients who really need to make lifestyle changes for the sake of their health may not be motivated by instructions and recommendations. But using stories to connect them emotionally with what they stand to gain or lose can be convincing and life-changing.

Ideas on How to Educate within the Framework of Stories

Use patients' own stories as a framework – Since your patients are going through a challenging chapter in their life stories, present education as part of the flow of their stories. Direct your education initiatives into the context of their real lives.

In your mind, outline the common storylines for the types of patients you deal with so you can better understand their personal perspectives and can direct your educational interventions more strategically within them. When possible, educate during the key medical interventions of their experiences rather than trying to educate them about everything at once or randomly. They will be much more interested in learning if the education fits into the trajectory of their stories.

Also, get patients to tell you what is happening with them during consultations or class discussions. Consider what they tell you as insight into their stories. When they tell their stories, you can understand them better because they'll show you what's important to them and what expectations they have. Seek to understand them and empathize with them so you can deal with them in relation to their actual feelings and issues. They are not just bodies that need mechanical fixing. Their stories give you the chance to clarify their roles within their care and how they can affect their health. Educate in the context of their narratives, and show how you are working in partnership with them to direct the plot of these stories.

Know the purpose of the stories – When you incorporate stories into your consultations and educational initiatives, plan them strategically ahead of time. Make sure you know the purpose of your stories and how they will help patients learn specific information or be affected in other positive ways

Show the process of care as a narrative – When you are preparing a presentation, new materials, videos, or website developments, use a narrative framework. Present the process of care in a narrative form since it already has that progressive structure. As you explain, take them along the natural flow of care and personalize it for them. You can offer this type of framework if you are:

- Describing the care process in a consultation or presentation
- Writing the patient guide
- Showing patients around the medical center or a unit
- Explaining surgery and treatment options as real choices that can affect the trajectory of their care
- Preparing patients for surgeries or treatments and what they can expect during and after the experiences
- Creating a video

Refer to known stories – You don't always need to find or create stories to teach concepts. Make references to common stories they already know, to historic or current events, or to familiar processes in nature or everyday life.

Encourage interactions – In group teaching sessions and patient conferences, encourage interaction with questions and discussion. Patients will often tell bits of their stories during their questions and comments. Other patients then hear these stores and relate to them, so this interaction helps all attendees to see their own stories in better perspective.

Get patients to tell their stories to others – At group sessions or patient conferences, arrange for two or three selected patients to tell their stories of medical challenges and treatments. The other patients who hear these testimonies tend to listen very closely and identify with much of what they are saying. You can arrange patient testimonies as a panel with a moderator asking prepared questions, or you can arrange for each patient to give a short presentation of their stories. Select patients with the types of stories you want presented, and then coach them on which points you'd like them to emphasize. Patient stories, photos, and quotations also work well to add a patient-centered focus to your presentations, websites, and publications. Many current and former patients tend to be very keen to participate by telling their stories.

Offer details – Some of your stories may just be a narrative backdrop that helps the flow of concepts, but other stories may represent real human drama with key decisions and outcomes. Offer enough detail, description, and sensory input so the stories are engaging, meaningful, and memorable. Good storytellers reveal the sights, sounds, smells, tastes, and feelings that surround and support the progressive action. Decide what to include, what to highlight, and what to leave out. If the emotional dimension of the story is important, make sure to include details that resonate with their feelings. Most of your stories will be short and directed to make a point, but there may be times for telling longer stories during presentations to create more impact.

Use photos – Use photos often because they are powerful storytellers. Photos can illustrate stories, and some of them tell stories by what they show. Use photos within all types of education initiatives – consultations, presentations, classes, websites, and materials. Photos can show real life images that help connect the medical information to their experiences. You can purchase great photos without much cost from stock photography sources. Or you can arrange for a photographer to take photos of what you want to show. You can get volunteers to act as patients as you set up and photograph many types of patient care experiences or lifestyle shots. Make sure that your photos are well-taken and clear.

Make videos – Videos are one of the best ways to tell stories since they have movement and can show almost anything to make your stories insightful, interesting, and compelling. Here are some of the types of stories you can tell in videos to help educate your patients:
- Virtual tours of how to navigate care at medical centers
- The patient experience of having certain tests, procedures, surgeries and treatments
- How to perform self-care procedures
- Current and former patients talking about their experiences
- Strategies for making important lifestyle changes
- Health care providers offering insight into health issues and treatments
- Dramas that show the important roles of patients and families in affecting health and outcomes
- Animations that show how the body functions, how injuries and diseases affect it, and how surgeries and treatments work to help it

You can make simple videos without professional equipment and training, but get professionals involved for any major productions.

Use medical records as stories – The medical records of your patients are the ongoing stories of their health care. If possible, consider giving patients access to their medical records, either electronically or in print. Organize the information so they can see the progression and understand their own medical stories better. You doctors will generally have more access to these records than other educators, so you may be able to lead out with this narrative approach.

Rather than just giving patients a pile of test results and some complex medical notes that they don't understand, organize the records to show the flow of consultations and treatments. Make clear notes so they understand the issues and interventions that make up their stories. When possible, show how their participation in their care makes a difference, such as how increased exercise results in lower blood sugar levels and lower blood pressure. Work with programmers and data specialists to develop interfaces that show patient records in this way.

Narrative Medicine

Some medical schools are teaching classes in narrative medicine based on evidence that stories have the power to improve care. In these classes, doctors learn to understand and relate to the life experiences of their patients. They learn to ask questions that encourage patients to tell the most important stories about their health, their current problems, their fears and their hopes. The doctors make detailed notes to record these stories and then learn to treat them in the context of these stories. Since the patients reveal much through their stories, the doctors learn a lot about treating patients as full human beings rather than just bodies. Most doctors who have tried this approach report great benefits and improved outcomes.[5]

It's Your Story Too

As a health care provider, your work and life is an unfolding story too, and your decisions affect the plot line. You want to be a great character and an effective healer who is liked and respected by patients and peers. You want to offer information and treatments that benefit the lives of many patients. You may want to be a hero who makes discoveries, demonstrates integrity, raises standards, and leaves an admirable legacy. You want to make others healthy and happy. You want your story to be an inspiration to those who connect with you now, and for those who will follow you later.

---

[5] Charon, R. (2001) Narrative Medicine: A model for empathy, reflection, profession and trust. JAMA, 286 (15) 1897 – 1902.

You can make your story better by interacting well with the stories of your patients. So, connect with the real lives of your patients, engage with them and educate them in relation to their minds, emotions, and spirits, as well as their bodies. When you enlighten your patients, you empower them to actively and effectively participate in their care, which often leads to higher satisfaction and better outcomes. Keep your own story in mind as you play a leading character in the stories of your patients.

The Best Ways to Educate

Your Patients

The Keys to Good Consultations
Best for Laying the Foundations of Learning

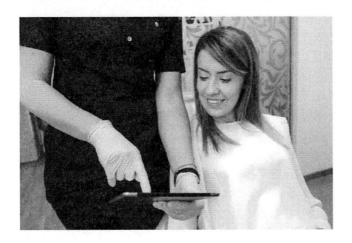

Consultations with patients are at the core of educating them well. Since consultations are private, personal, and focused, you have the best opportunities to interact with patients and to teach them the essential details about their health problems and potential solutions. But your time with patients is limited during these interactions, so you cannot teach them everything they may need to know. They will most likely need supplementary materials, computer links, classes, or other education options to flesh out their understanding, but you can provide the most potent part of their education. How you explain and discuss information with them will largely determine their response to learning and how much they are motivated to participate effectively in their care.

You may not be the one who consults directly with patients. If not, then do whatever you can to help enhance the consultations of those who do connect with patients in this way. Consultations are a key component of the whole education initiative.

Here are some suggestions to help make the most of opportunities to educate patients well during consultations:

Partner with patients for their care – If you want to empower patients, you should approach them and treat them as partners with you in helping to resolve health issues. If you present yourself as the life-giving hero and talk to them as helpless invalids, then you create a full dependence on you and the medical center. Patients will not feel they have the knowledge or ability to do anything, so they will be coming back to you for every concern and every bit of care, using up time and resources. They may also hold you and the center more responsible for desired or undesired outcomes. There certainly are procedures and treatments that require patients to be fully dependent on you for a time, but do whatever you can to get them to partner with you through most of their care.

Treat them with value and respect – Patients come to you because you have the qualifications and expertise to help them deal with their health challenges. To gain their trust and respect, treat them well. Always recognize and speak to the value, intelligence, and human dignity of those you are treating. You may have the advantage of knowing how to treat their medical problems, but you are not above them in the broader context of life. These patients come to you with a rich collection of education and experience, hope and desires, stresses and disappointments, hard losses and great gains. Some of them are also medical professionals. Whether they are professionals or not, rich or poor, young or old, they come to you with the full value of being a human being, equal to yourself.

Start off well – When you first enter consult rooms to see new patients, start off by doing all of the following:
- Smile – it does not need to be a big smile, but a positive expression.
- State their names to show that you have taken time to look at their records and know who they are. Ask them what name they want you to call them since some may have a preference other than their official name.
- Introduce yourself – your name and your title or role as it relates to their care.
- If other care providers such as nurses or students enter with you, introduce the other care providers and get them to identify their roles.
- If there are family members or others with the patients, also greet them, ask their names and find out how they are connected with the patients.
- Show human warmth and genuine care in your approach.

- Demonstrate a full respect for them as intelligent and valuable human beings who are partners with you in their care.

Clarify their health problems and interventions – Many patients may be confused about the names and nature of their exact problems. So set the foundation for their education this way:

- **Name their health problems** – Give them the names of their problems in both verbal and written form, unless it is something as obvious as a simple bone fracture. Some medical conditions have more than one name, a common name and a medical term. Make sure they have both names, and let them know that they refer to the same problem.
- **Describe their health problems** – Concisely and clearly describe their problems to them, ideally using visual aids such as charts, drawings, models, or electronic images. Show where the problem is located in their bodies and how it is affecting their bodies. If the problems are potentially progressive, with or without treatments, explain the possible progression and its effects on their bodies.
- **Name and describe their surgeries and treatments** – After clarifying their health problems, move on to describing and discussing the solutions – their treatment options.
    - For some conditions, there is one clear way to treat them, so you don't need to get into a detailed discussion about options. Just explain their treatment, give them a chance to ask questions, and provide them with supplementary materials or links, if appropriate.
    - If there is more than one option for treating patients, give them the names of their surgery or treatment options, and describe each one clearly. If they have a range of options, help them to understand these options in relation to the problems and to each other.
    - If patients really have a choice between options, then empower them to make their choices, and give them the essential details to make informed decisions. Don't skip over things that they may learn later and cause them to second-guess their decisions.
    - If you are recommending one option over others, make sure

85

to clearly explain why you are recommending it over the other options in your evidence-based approach.

- o Always check to make sure they understand your descriptions and explanations, and give them the chance to ask questions and get direct answers.
- **Give them materials or links for reference** – To supplement your discussion of their health problems and possible solutions, give them information for reference and further learning. Even if you are giving them a computer link, give them printed connection instructions. Patients tend to forget much of what you say in consultations, so they really need information to remind them of the discussion and to learn even more.

Relate to their stories – As discussed in the chapter *How to Use Stories to Educate Patients*, the lives of your patients are stories, and their health challenges are chapters in their stories. All learning works best in the framework of their stories. Otherwise, the information may seem so detached that they choose to ignore it because they don't see how it fits into their real lives.

To educate in relation to their stories, listen to them. Ask them questions, hear what they are saying, read their body language, and let them express their confusion, concerns, and desires. Studies in narrative medicine show the significant advantages of this approach for both patients and care providers. When you understand their stories, you can relate to them, educate them, and treat them better. Take all their comments and all aspects of their stories seriously as you build an understanding and rapport with them. The result is more satisfied patients, better outcomes and benefits for you and the medical center.

Get patients involved in their care – Most patients don't want to be helpless and dependent on their health care providers for all aspects of care. Most want to play important roles themselves, so let them know your role and their roles as you partner with them for their care.

- If they need to take medications, let them know how the medications work to help them so they will be more likely to take them.
- If they need to learn more about some topics, direct their

learning by giving them materials, website links, or other options.

- If they need to learn a self-care procedure, such as wound care, offer them instructions, demonstrations, illustrated materials, web links, or videos. If the procedure has any complexity, make sure they have a chance to demonstrate their competence and ask questions.
- If they need to make lifestyle changes, appeal to their emotions as well as their minds to convince them of the importance of these changes for their healing and health. Direct them to further learning such as counselling or classes to help them learn more about making changes. See the chapter on *How to Get Patients to Participate in Their Care.*

Be direct and honest – One of the main reasons to educate patients is to give them the facts. They need to know the reality of their health problems and possible solutions. Let patients deal with the reality of their situation rather than leading them on with false hopes, or letting them discover bad news in other ways. As a fellow human being, you owe your patients the truth you have discovered about their bodies so they and their families can best work together for healing or for palliative care. Show your own human empathy and compassion in difficult situations, and refer them to other supportive care, when appropriate.

Always end with words about next steps – When you are finished your consultations with patients, always let them know about the next steps in their care. Don't just walk out and leave them wondering what will happen next. Even if a nurse or someone else will give them further instructions, let patients know who will provide them with further instructions. Otherwise, patients may feel that they have been disconnected or abandoned. If their care involves a process, give them a brief overview of what types of tests, treatments, visits or other care they can expect and how they will know about these appointments. End with a positive expression and a few nurturing words. If you will be seeing them again, your nurturing words can be a quick comment about continuing care at their next appointment with you.

Follow through well – If you will be seeing patients more than once, make sure to remember them, build rapport, and keep your commitments to them.

- Call them by whatever name they want to be called.
- Make clear notes in your files so you remember and refer to what you discussed at previous consultations.
- Make sure to follow through on what you say you will do. If you don't, you lose their trust, confidence, and respect.
- Keep them engaged in learning. The more patients know, the more empowered they become. As the care progresses, so does the need to learn more information. Teach them yourself, or direct them to other sources of learning. Learning can become a positive way to engage and help them feel good about the progress of their care.
- Remember that you are now an important character in their stories, so be attentive, personable, caring, and as positive as possible. Be a good human as well as health care provider. Offer the best of yourself for the best of them.

Printed Documents
Best for Supplementing Consultations

Offer printed materials – If good materials already exist, use them. If you can't find appropriate materials, develop your own. Most likely you will need to develop some materials to reflect the unique treatments and process of care that you provide at your medical center. Some of the benefits of offering printed documents include:

- Printed materials are excellent ways to help educate patients since they offer a familiar and tangible way for them to learn.
- If printed materials are well developed with clear language, good organization, and lots of illustrations, they make learning easy for most patients.
- Printed materials can be developed to offer a brief overview of essential information, or they can offer extensive information for those who need or want to learn more.

Types of printed materials – You can select to use one or several types of materials

- Information cards
- Handout sheets
- Pamphlets – 2-fold, 3-fold, 4-fold
- Booklets
- Books – generally ones they can borrow from a library or learning center

Distribution – Coordinate a systematic way to distribute printed materials to patients. Here are some ways:

- Give directly as part of care – Offer materials directly to patients at consultations or other interactions. All patients should get documents that reflect their health issues, treatments, and other care. Don't give them too much at once but bit by bit as it integrates with the care they are receiving.
- Provide materials to patients as handouts at group learning sessions as a reference and extension of the content presented.
- Distribute in pamphlet racks – Make optional materials on a wide variety of topics available in pamphlet racks at selected locations. These racks can contain not only pamphlets but information sheets, information cards, and booklets as well. Make sure the racks have the following characteristics:
  o Big enough for a wide selection of materials, as appropriate to the types of patients in each area.
  o Clear enough so patients can see the full titles of all materials. Purchased or custom made racks of clear acrylic work well.
  o Deep enough slots for lots of materials, but not so deep that the materials fall over – 3 to 5 centimeters (2 to 3 inches) works well in most cases.
  o Attractive – Select racks that are attractive and fit well into the layout and décor.
  o Well-maintained – Make sure the racks are filled regularly so there are rarely empty slots or out-of-date materials. You may be able to arrange for trained volunteers to fill them. Patients and promoters tend to put their own materials in the racks to

promote products or ideas, so you will need to watch for and discard unwanted additions.

Ordering, storing and managing materials – Develop a workable and systematic way to order, store, and manage printed materials. There are various ways to deal with materials, but consider the following options:

- Designate a coordinator – If possible, hire a materials coordinator if you work at a big medical center, or designate this role to somebody who can focus on it part time. This role is probably too big and intensive for a volunteer, unless your center is small and uses limited materials.
- Get an on-site storage area – If possible, arrange to have an on-site storage area big enough to organize and store materials for regular distribution. There are two ways to get the materials from storage to the clinical distribution areas:
  - Designate somebody to take the materials to each distribution area, as needed. You can set up an internal electronic ordering system.
  - Or arrange for each department to come to the storage area to get the materials they need. If they are coming to get materials, organize and label the storage area in a very clear way so they can find whatever they need.
- Code materials – Code and date internally-produced materials for easy ordering and management. It works best to set up an electronic database of all materials with clear ordering procedures.
- Control inventory – Calculate distribution and usage rates of all materials so whoever is managing materials can order and keep adequate supplies available at all times. Work out a way to keep track of current supplies.
- Order big supplies – If you are ordering volumes of materials from outside sources, order big supplies that will last for several months. Many organizations only print at certain times, so they don't always have supplies on hand for urgent requests. If you are getting your own materials printed, printers usually offer volume discounts.

Patient Classes and Other Sessions
Best for Educating Many Patients
Efficiently and Effectively

Consider offering a variety of learning sessions – There are 6 main types of group sessions:

- Orientation sessions
- Classes
- Self-care training and practice sessions
- Special presentations
- Patient conferences and symposiums
- Web-accessed live or recorded sessions – may be electronic versions of any of the types listed above, or sessions planned specifically for website teaching

The benefits of group sessions – Group learning sessions are an excellent way to educate many patients effectively and efficiently. If you have many patients who need to learn similar information, it makes good sense to teach them as groups. Group sessions can be optional, or you can schedule patients into them as an educational intervention that is part of their care. Group sessions offer several learning advantages for patients:

- Since most sessions feature a presenter with slide and/or video support, patients can both hear and see information which creates interest and helps them remember.
- Many patients like having concepts explained to them, so these sessions offer them an easy way to learn.
- Sessions are generally interactive so the patients can ask questions and get answers. This interaction helps learning, plus patients often gain insight from each other during the discussions.
- Family members and other companions are usually involved with patient care to some degree. By encouraging them to attend sessions, they learn along with the patients and can thereby understand the information and help the patients better.

Orientation Sessions

What to include at orientations – At smaller medical centers, orientations are usually short and personal. But large outpatient centers with similar types of patients may benefit by offering group orientations since they can empower patients from the beginning and create efficiencies in the process of their care. Some topics and features to consider for orientation sessions:

- Warm welcome
- Important facts and features about the medical center
- Commitment of the center to providing quality care to patients
- Description of key departments and services
- Navigation information to main departments and services, including amenities – good idea to show maps, floor plans and photos – consider offering them a virtual tour or a real tour as part of the session
- The process and experience of patient care – use lots of photo or video images to show the experiences
- Main treatments and how they work – a brief overview
- How they can actively participate in their care as partners along with the health care team – defined roles for both
- The benefits of learning and their options for education at the medical center
- Some encouraging words about dealing with health challenges in the context of life
- Testimonies and experiences of current or former patients. You can show photos and quotes from patients on slides, or you can show a short video of patients talking about their experiences, or you can even arrange to have volunteer patients come in to tell their stories for a few minutes.

How to make orientations work well:

- There are two ways to get patients to attend orientation sessions:
  - Schedule patients into them as part of their care.
  - Or promote them in a very compelling way so many will be motivated to come.

- Orientation presenters should be warm, friendly, engaging, professional, genuine, and knowledgeable. You may choose to have more than one presenter.
- To make them worth attending, orientation sessions should be at least an hour long, but can go up to an hour and a half with time for interactive discussion.
- Also offer patients a printed or electronic patient guide, which has similar information to the orientation. In light of this guide, the live sessions should offer more information, interesting visual slides, special features, interaction, and very personable and caring presenters. The orientation should be much more than verbal navigation instructions.
- You can record an orientation session and feature it on your website. But few patients will watch anything longer than 20 minutes, and the recording loses a lot of the benefits of a live introductory session.

Classes

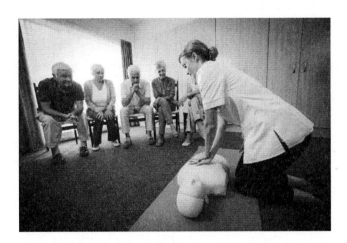

Consider the following points of insight and suggestions regarding classes:

Effective – Just like schools and universities are able to teach many students through classes, you will find that they work well for educating your patients too.

Efficient – Many care providers repeat the same information over and over again to each new patient, taking up time, energy, and resources. You can create efficiencies by scheduling similar types of patients into classes where they can all learn together. Classes can be very impactful, especially with good presenters since patients hear the information clearly and see the key points and illustrations on slides.

Timeframes – The ideal time for classes is around 1 ½ hours. This allows for a 1 hour presentation and ½ hour for discussion. If patients make an effort to come to classes, offer enough content and practical information to make them worthwhile. Patients tend to like early to mid-afternoon class times best. Mornings can work well too if they are scheduled no earlier than 10 AM. You don't want your patients to travel during the morning traffic rush if you can prevent it. Evening classes get some response, but they are generally not as popular as afternoon sessions. Older patients tend to dislike going out at night for sessions, but evenings work well for some younger patients who work during the day.

Frequency – The frequency of the classes will depend on the size of your medical center and the numbers of patients who come for care. They can be as frequent as every day or as infrequent as once every few months. You can increase or decrease the frequency depending on demand and logistics.

Required and optional classes – Most medical centers can help patients and families by offering several classes, some optional and others that are scheduled appointments. Promote optional classes in compelling ways to get patients to come. Refer to the chapter in this book called *How to Promote Education Programs to Get Participation*. If you are scheduling patients into classes, do it through appropriate channels and communicate clearly. You may choose to work with booking clerks to make this happen.

Venues – Use the best spaces available for each class, and ensure everything is well arranged and set up before the patients arrive.
- Large medical centers usually have an auditorium or classrooms that may be used primarily by staff and medical students. Find out the current usage schedule of these teaching areas and

reserve time for group learning sessions.

- All medical centers have patient waiting areas. These waiting areas can be turned into classrooms after regular clinic hours, and sometimes even during clinic hours. They already have chairs and may have a media screen that can work for presentation slides. At designated times, arrange the chairs so the whole space works well for group learning sessions.

Presenters – When possible, choose presenters who are engaging as well as established professionals. If a presenter is boring, too complex, or seems unsure of the content, patients will lose interest, learn little, and regret coming. Some presenters can be mentored into being better communicators.

For regular sessions, generally arrange presenters from within your medical center. Even if they have other roles, you can likely recruit them to teach classes occasionally. But also consider using experts from the community to teach certain topics, where appropriate. You may need to pay outside experts for their services

Handouts – Generally plan and prepare to offer patients supplementary handouts when they come to classes. The handouts should offer them a reference to the information taught in the class, as well as content, links and/or recommendations for further learning.

Topics – The range of topics for classes is as broad as the types of health issues your medical center addresses. Set up classes that will benefit the most patients in the most ways. Here are a few topic suggestions. Try to create specific and compelling class names:

- The Benefits of Eating Well
  - Other names: The Power of Nutrition; Eating for Your Life
- The Benefits of Being Physically Active
  - Other names: The Power of Exercise; Exercising for Your Life
- Complementary Therapy Options for _____ (insert any condition or disease)
- Help to Manage Fatigue
- Help to Manage Pain
- Help to Manage _____ (insert any condition or disease)

- Preparing for _____ Surgery (insert any type of surgery)
- Recovering from _____Surgery (insert any type of surgery)
- Preparing for _____Treatments (insert any type of treatments)
- Learn to _____ at Home (insert any type of self-care procedure)

Schedules – When you have several classes planned, develop promotional descriptions and monthly schedules to give patients. The more your promotions stand out, the more response you will get. These promotions should be in print, but they can also be promoted at orientation sessions, your websites, and on digital information screens.

Pre-Registration – If possible, plan an easy way for your patients to sign up for optional classes. When they sign up, they are more committed to attending, plus you have an idea of how many are planning to come. Don't insist that they must all sign up online since some people don't have access or the ability. If possible, give them the choice to call a real person to pre-register. You don't need to get patients to pre-register if you have enough space for all those who might come. If you don't require pre-registration, make sure the promotion clearly states that they should just show up since pre-registration is not required.

Special Presentations

The role for special sessions – Offer special presentations to keep your education initiatives fresh and diverse, and to interest patients in gaining new information on compelling topics.

- Take advantage of opportunities to feature hot topics and new speakers. For example, your medical center may have doctors from other cities and countries coming to offer presentations to staff. Since these leading experts are coming to your center anyway, arrange for them to give a patient presentation as well. Since the medical center may already be paying the expenses of these experts, you may get them to present at no extra cost.
- Also seek out and invite presenters from the medical center,

community, and supportive organizations. If you don't have a budget to pay them or their expenses, then you will be more limited in whom you can invite, but many will present at little or no cost, as they are supported to do so by their own organizations.

- Make sure to clearly arrange all details with the presenters ahead of time so the topics, audience, time, location, and expectations have been clearly discussed and confirmed.
- Promote to patients in whatever way you can. If it is a compelling topic or speaker, make sure to promote it that way on posters, digital screens, your websites, and whatever way you can.
- If you don't have a good way to pre-register attendees, then leave it open and arrange to have enough space for as many as may choose to come. If it is open, make sure to let them know that they can just show up.

Patient Conferences

Description and purpose – Patient conferences can be planned and coordinated in whatever way works best for you and your patients. These types of sessions are sometimes referred to as *symposiums*. They generally feature several presentations and discussions on a specific topic, or on several topics relevant to certain types of patients. For example, some conferences can be about such things as pain management for those with chronic pain, and others can feature many topics of interest for breast cancer patients. These sessions allow you to educate and nurture groups of patients to give them a boost of special enlightenment and empowerment.

Times – Patient conferences can range from about 3 hours to 2 days. A 4 hour afternoon conference is ideal since it allows enough time for several features, but it's not so long that you need to coordinate extensive logistics. Determine the length, days, and timeframes that will work best for your patients and professional participants.

Consider holding conferences on Friday afternoons. You may not have considered holding a major learning session on a Friday afternoon, but there are several reasons why this timeframe works well:

- Venues are often more open for booking during this timeframe next to weekends, so it's easier to find space.
- Doctors and other staff members tend to have more open schedules at this time, so it's usually easier to get them to participate. It also saves them from coming to present in the evenings or weekends.
- Patients who have jobs may find it more convenient to leave work at noon on Fridays than at other times during the week.

Who needs to be involved – Some conferences are small and may be put together and run by an experienced staff member with good connections and support. But most conferences require several professionals to be involved and to play important roles. Here is a list and description of who generally needs to be involved:

- **Conference coordinator** – This person leads in planning and running the conference.
- **Planning committee** – A committee is not always necessary, but input from key staff and patients can enhance the focus and nature of the conference.
- **Conference moderator** – A central personality who will offer a welcome, introduce speakers, give instructions and present a friendly face and consistency to the conference. In some cases, the coordinator may also be the moderator.
- **Volunteers** – Volunteers are very valuable in taking on such tasks as getting supplies to the conference, welcoming attendees, handing out packages, directing and assisting attendees, and cleaning up afterwards.
- **Professional presenters** – Professional presenters provide the main conference content. Recruit the best internal and external presenters to offer the most interesting and helpful information. The success of the conference largely depends on the ability of the presenters to engage with the attendees by presenting compelling information and by using language, concepts, and visuals that patients can understand.

- **Patient presenters** – Patients really like to hear the stories of other patients dealing with similar issues. Arrange to have two or three patients give their testimonies either as short presentations or as part of a panel. Ask front line care providers at your medical center to select patients who have had positive experiences and may be able to offer practical insight. Ask these patients to participate, and then coach them on your expectations. These testimonies tend to be one of the favorite parts of conferences for attendees.
- **Technical support** – Make sure to have attentive technical support for conferences to set up the equipment and keep the microphones and all of the equipment running well. Conferences can easily be spoiled by technical issues. Ensure that whoever is providing support has extra bulbs, batteries, and equipment for easy resolutions to issues. If the session is going to be video-conferenced to other locations, do whatever possible to plan these links well so connection issues don't distract from the live experience for local attendees or disappoint those at other locations.

The parts of a conference – You have flexibility in choosing what to include in each conference, but you should generally plan for the following components:
- **Welcome**
  - Provided by the moderator
  - Warm and friendly in nature
  - Sets the focus and tone
  - Offers a quick overview of what to expect
  - Gives necessary instructions, including encouragement to fill out the evaluation form
  - Prepare a special slide or slides as background for the welcome
- **Presentations**
  - A selection of professional and patient presenters provide the main content of the conference.
  - Most presentations should have visual support, such as slides or demonstrations, so patients can see as well as hear the information.
  - Most professional presentations should be from 20 to 40

minutes long. If presenters have lots of content, schedule them for more than one presentation with another presenter in between.

- o Consider including the following types of presentations:
  - Health problem 101 – an overview of the specific health problems or issues featured
  - The most effective current surgeries and treatments for the health problems
  - The latest updates on research and new treatment developments
  - Information on available support and resources to help them cope, connect, get assistance, and make changes
  - Patient testimonies offering real life insight into the health issues and treatments – generally limited to 10 to 15 minutes each, or arranged as a panel discussion

- **Discussions and panels**
  - o Attendees want and need a chance to ask questions and discuss the featured topics, so plan specific time for these interactions. You can arrange for presenters to have extra time right at the end of their presentations, or you can arrange for a panel discussion where several presenters come to the front together to take questions and provide insight after they have all presented.
  - o For most conferences encourage attendees to put up their hands to indicate they would like to speak. If the space is large, get volunteers to offer roving microphones to those who want to speak so everyone can hear the questions and comments.
  - o In some cases, it works best to have attendees write out their questions on cards provided to them. Volunteers then pick up these cards and hand them to the presenter or moderator. This approach can work well for a panel discussion. The moderator then selects and reads questions to the panel members for a response. But when possible, let the attendees verbalize their own questions and comments since attendees like to hear the voices of others in attendance.
  - o Panel discussions can also work well as learning features, adding some interactive variety and dynamics. Arrange for a group of professionals or patients to come up front together

and be directed in discussion by a moderator. They may be able to offer a spectrum of insight on a featured topic and interact with each other in interesting and insightful ways. For these types of panels, try getting the panel members to offer their featured insight first, and then welcome interaction from attendees.

- **Breaks and refreshments**
  - Plan for breaks about every hour and a half
  - Offer drinks at all breaks – generally water, small bottles or cartons of fruit juice, coffee, and herbal teas
  - Offer some food at one break if the conference is more than 3 hours long. Include some protein selections since attendees generally need some substance to feel good. If you have an extended conference, you will need to arrange for full meals, generally provided by a caterer, or by the hotel or conference center.
  - If the conference is small, then short breaks of about 15 minutes are enough. But if you have many attendees and a selection of refreshments, plan for 30 minute breaks and an hour for meal times.
- **Videos**
  - You don't need to show videos, but they add another dimension to the sessions by providing such features as virtual tours, demonstrations, insight from leading experts, narratives, music, and inspiration.
- **Exhibits**
  - Add to the learning options of the conference by arranging for exhibits that feature such things as information, products, support, and equipment related to the topics of discussion.
  - Attendees like to visit these exhibits before the conference begins and during the breaks.
  - For more insight on preparing exhibits, see the section on *Information Exhibits and Fairs.*
- **Conclusion**
  - Provided by the moderator.
  - Keep it short and positive.
  - Offer a quick summary of the session and a positive focus on the future.
  - Thank all presenters, volunteers, sponsors (if any), and

attendees for coming.
- o Encourage attendees to turn in their evaluation forms at the back as they leave.
- o Wish them well.

Conference Planning Checklist

Here is a checklist to help you plan and coordinate conferences strategically. The order of your planning may vary from the sequence of this list.

- [ ] Bring together a **conference committee**.
  - Select the most appropriate stakeholders to join.
  - Consider including one or more patients on the committee.
  - Work together to plan the conference details, but keep the planning moving quickly and strategically.
  - There are cases where a committee may not be necessary such as:
    - When the planned conferences are small or limited in scope with a very defined agenda.
    - In centers where a well-connected coordinator has had lots of prior experience arranging such sessions.
- [ ] Determine **conference audience**.
  - Types of patients and others who will benefit most.
  - Estimate realistic numbers of how many will attend.
- [ ] Determine **conference objectives** and how to best meet them.
  - List the specific ways you want this learning event to benefit the patients and family members who attend.
  - Discuss what presentations and other features would help meet these objectives best.

- [ ] Choose conference **topic and name**.
- [ ] Choose conference **coordinator**.
- [ ] Choose conference **moderator**.
- [ ] Arrange for conference **funding**.

- Estimate costs for all aspects – promotion, venue, equipment, materials, catering, and speakers.
- Unless already funded, plan to access or solicit funding.
- If sponsorship is a consideration, decide on who may sponsor and in what way.
- See the chapter on *How to Access Funding.*
- Confirm funding before moving ahead with detailed planning, booking and promoting.

☐ Choose a **date and timeframe** for the conference and confirm it.

☐ Book best available **venue**, including chairs, tables, and needed equipment.

☐ Book **technical support**.

☐ Decide what types of presentations and other features to offer, then **book and confirm all presenters**.

- Develop a preliminary schedule before you book presenters so you can let them know how you'd like them to fit into the flow of the event.
- Confirm in writing the specific topic, name of presentation, location, and timeframe of each presenter and presentation.
- Give clear instructions on how to send the media slides ahead of time for loading on the conference computer. It works best to have all presentations loaded ahead of time to enable smooth transitions between presenters.
- If the presenters are not local staff, then arrange all necessary travel details with each presenter, including such things as fees or honorariums, travel costs, flights, hotels, transportation, and parking.

☐ Decide what types of exhibits to arrange, then **book and confirm all exhibitors**.

- Coordinate details clearly with all exhibitors ahead of the event. They need to know the exact location, set up and take down times, active display times, and your expectations.
- Encourage those who have displays to make them as interesting, attractive, and interactive as possible.

☐ **Create a final schedule** to use for promotions and to give attendees.

☐ Plan for the help of **volunteers,** then solicit and schedule these volunteers in specific roles.

☐ Decide on what **refreshments** to offer during breaks and how to get those refreshments. Then order catering, or make other arrangements for refreshments.

☐ Make a plan on how to **promote the event**, and then prepare and direct the promotions.
  - See chapter on *How to Promote Education Programs to Get Participation*

☐ Develop a simple **evaluation form** to give attendees at the event.

☐ Decide what to give attendees in a **conference package** and plan how to acquire these documents. Near the event date, prepare the packages to give out, including final schedule, evaluation form, and possibly copies of the presentation slides. Arrange for volunteers to help.

☐ Create a **welcome slide** to display on the screen while attendees enter.

☐ Coordinator **sets up** on the day of conference.

- Displays direction signage to the event using posters, signboards, or digital screens.
- Arranges for all materials and equipment to be taken to the venue.
- Arrives at the venue at least one or two hours before the start time to take care of all setup details.

- Makes sure all chairs, tables, and equipment are arranged well.
- Works with technical support to check and test all equipment, set microphones sound levels, and to clarify all expectations.
- If possible, arranges for all presentation slides to be pre-loaded onto the conference computer before the event starts.
- Displays the welcome slide on the screen.
- Welcomes all volunteers and directs them in their roles.
- Welcomes all exhibitors and directs them in setting up their displays.
- Arranges for volunteers to welcome all attendees and give them a package of conference materials.
- Arranges refreshments for distribution.

☐ Coordinator and moderator work together to **run the conference**.

- Moderator offers welcome messages to attendees.
- Coordinator welcomes presenters personally when they arrive and confirms their presentation and discussion times.
- Coordinator and moderator work together to keep the presentations flowing according to the schedule. They may arrange to signal presenters when their time is nearly up, or may allow some flexibility for smaller or less formal events. Generally keep things close to the prepared schedule.
- Coordinator makes sure the refreshments are set up for distribution before each break.
- Coordinator and moderator work together to deal with any issues that arise since each conference has a life of its own, no matter how well it is planned.
- At the end of the conference, moderator offers concluding messages, including a reminder to hand in the evaluation form.

- ☐ Coordinator manages **wrap up** and **clean up**.
  - Coordinator works with volunteers to clean up and to return equipment and remaining supplies, if necessary.
  - Coordinator gathers evaluation forms and arranges for them to be analysed and summarized in a report.
  - Within two weeks of the event, the coordinator meets again with the committee for a debriefing where they discuss the evaluation report, determine how well the objectives were achieved, and determine how to make future conferences even better.

Websites

Best for Extending the Reach of Learning

Make a visible link to patient information – Your website is a powerful and expansive way to offer your patients clear information about the health care you provide. Since your website likely includes public and professional information as well as patient information, create a clear icon link to connect patients to the patient features.

Be nurturing – Create the patient features of your website in a warm, friendly, clear, and nurturing way. The titles and information should come across with the personality of an attentive care provider so that it seems more personal and helpful than other sites. Feature the expertise and approach of health care professionals in photos and videos so patients feel welcomed into the care setting whenever they go to your site.

Be clear – One of the biggest problems with most websites is that they are written in language that is beyond the understanding of many patients. Ensure that all content in the patient sections is written and spoken in plain language and organized in logical way for easy navigation. Refer to the chapter in this book called *Be Very Clear – Plain Language Guidelines.*

Be active – Continually update your website with new information to make it worth repeated visits. Some of the health care information may stay the same for a long time, but keep adding new features, news updates, and schedules of learning events.

Be accurate – You want your website information to be very reliable, so ensure that everything you add to the website is endorsed by health care providers at your medical center and reflects the care that you offer.

What to feature:

- Use your website to educate your patients in several ways, but use it as a supplement to more personal and more direct education options.
- Include an electronic version of your patient guide with all of the essential medical center and navigation information. You can include a PDF of your printed guide, but create an interactive web version if you can.
- Consider offering a virtual tour of your medical center with either photos or video.
- Include information on the health problems and treatments that you offer. Provide enough information so patients have a good general understanding of health issues since this may be the

first place they look for information. For those who may want more detailed information, such as treatment guidelines, offer them links or instructions on where they can find this information.

- Promote events and schedules of patient learning options in a clear and compelling way.
- Over time, offer several video selections on specific health information. You can feature these types of videos:
  o Mini-classes
  o Full classes, presentations and conference – you can include full recorded versions of the live programs at your center, but patients tend to not watch videos that are more than about 20 minutes.
  o Interviews with medical experts and patients
  o Patient testimonies and stories
  o Animations of medical treatments
  o Consultation explanations, if this will support and reduce consultation time
  o Videos showing patients in various care settings. These experience videos tend to ease fears about upcoming care.

Webinars – Webinars are live classes, presentations, and discussions that happen over the internet. Plan the sessions by making arrangements with website professionals for technical coordination, and then promote to patients so they connect from their home computers or smart phones. If well planned, promoted and coordinated, these webinars can work well to educate many patients on almost any topic. You can record the sessions and keep them featured on your site after the event.

Patient portals – Patient portals are becoming more popular, but each one is developed uniquely, so there is no world standard on the ideal way to create them. Patient portals are special sections of your website, or an associated website, that allow patients to do such things as:

- Access their medical records online
- Make appointments online
- Get prescriptions renewed

- Receive specific information related to their conditions and treatments
- Ask questions and get responses

These portals have a lot of potential, so they will continue to evolve to benefit patients in more ways. You don't need a portal to educate patients since education doesn't need to be restricted to special access sites, but portals can offer personal patient information that direct them to specific learning options. The information that you offer on portals can be targeted and prescriptive to specific patients or types of patients, and you are able to track what information has been accessed by the patients. Find ways to work with portal developers to enhance them for learning purposes.

Links to other websites – Since no website and no medical center can be all things for all patients, direct patients to other sources of information and help too. One of the best ways to do this is to identify, describe, and list all of these links in one section rather than having them scattered around your site. You are likely to lose patients to these other sites if they appear everywhere, but putting them all in one section may help keep them focused on your site until they are ready to look for outside information and support.

Videos
Best for Creating Interest and Impact

Advantages of videos – When possible, access videos and create videos to help educate your patients. Videos have several advantages:

- They educate well by appealing to both sight and hearing with lots of activity, visual insight, various voices, music, and other sounds. The more senses that you engage, the better the patients learn and the longer they remember.
- Patients usually like watching videos if they are well produced and if they offer interesting and practical information.
- They are popular and can be featured almost anywhere, as demonstrated by such sites as YouTube® and Facebook®.
- They are very versatile since you can teach and show almost anything by videos. They can be a simple recording of a patient or professional speaking to the camera, or they can be highly produced with sweeping footage, virtual tours, views inside bodies, animation, and other components that would be hard to visualize in any other way.
- You can use videos as a part of consultations or group sessions, as DVD's to hand out, and as features for websites and digital information screens.
- They are an excellent way to teach self-care procedures since demonstration is necessary to help patients learn how to perform them. Rather than staff demonstrating procedures for each patient, videos can do the job well and much more efficiently. However, patients should have a chance to ask questions and demonstrate competence after watching the videos.
- You can capture presentations and discussions with leading experts and other important events on videos, then use them to benefit patients for months and years to come.

Access good videos – Many high quality videos on various health topics have already been produced by medical organizations and companies. If they are appropriate and useful, access them and show them to patients, or direct your patients to sites where they can watch them. Your library or learning center may have paid access to sites that would otherwise cost you and your patients to watch.

Produce high quality videos – If you have funding, work with professional producers to create videos or a series of videos on key topics you want to feature. Since these productions are often expensive, get necessary input and approval for scripts and images so you don't have to make changes soon after production. Most videos need updating in time though, so keep that in mind for future budgets.

Produce easy videos – Making videos does not need to be a difficult or expensive initiative. Most cameras and smartphones can shoot video footage, and there are several programs that make editing easy. A lot of meeting rooms have equipment that will record sessions for you when you push a button. Use the best cameras and professionals that you can, but do what you can with the resources available. Use videos in many aspects of education for interest and impact.

Let patients record consultations and demonstrations – Since most patients and family members now carry smartphones with them, let them record important consultations, instructions, and demonstrations, if they wish. For example, family members may record nurses showing patients the complex procedures for dressings or ostomy care so they can refer to this specific information at home. You may want to encourage patients and families to record some things.

Digital Information Screens
Best for Catching Attention and Informing Patients While they Wait

Install screens – If possible, install digital information screens in all main patient waiting areas. Install them so they are very visible in each waiting area, but don't make them so obtrusive that they can't be ignored by those who don't want to watch. These screens get lots of attention and they can be an effective way to help educate patients.

Screen content – Here are suggestions for the types of information that works well to inform and educate patients:

- Key facts about health problems and treatments
- Key facts about the medical center
- Key messages for patients about navigation and care
- Interesting information about life and health
- Encouragement to make helpful lifestyle changes
- Key facts about nutrition and exercise
- Tips or suggestions about almost anything related to health
- Medical professionals offering insight
- Patients talking about positive experiences
- Promotion for all patient education programs
- Encouragement and inspiration
- Pop up announcements, such as a message about a delay in appointment times on a given day
- Medical news
- Promising medical research updates
- Interludes of soft music with relaxing images

Logistics – The content prepared from these screens needs to come from a computer or a server. If you have many screens to coordinate, they all need to be connected to a controlling server which makes these connections easy to manage. Unless you are a technical expert yourself, you will need professionals to install, connect, and program the equipment. Ideally, the whole system is already set up so you can collaborate with those who set it up and find ways to educate patients on the system. At large centers with many types of patients, you may want to feature some unique content in each area for each main type of patient.

Rotation of content – Keep the screen content rotating about every 15 to 30 minutes. If you have limited content to begin with, the rotations can be shorter, but if the same topics appear every few minutes, your patients may find them irritating.

Sharing – Unless you have received special funding for these screens, you will probably be sharing them with other departments, such as foundations or public relations who also have messages for patients. If so, find ways to work together for a good balance and flow of messages.

Keep screens mostly silent – Most of the time, these screens should be silent or with only soft, relaxing music in the background. Patients find it very irritating to have voices blaring out at them for a long time. So create the content to be captivating with images and printed words on the screen rather than voiced videos. If somebody is talking, just include the flowing captions at the bottom. Don't have too many words on the screen at any given time.

Preparing content – At a basic level, you can create content for these screens with electronic slides like you do for presentations. Limit the number of words on each slide and include lots of images. Beyond slides, you can make videos to add to the rotation loop. Going further, seek out special programs that can help you create content attractively and professionally, or work with media specialists who can do this for you. Also, many health organizations and companies now produce great videos and animations for these screens that you can purchase or use.

Libraries and Learning Centers
Best for Books and Electronic Access to Quality Health Information

Libraries – Patient libraries offer various types of printed and electronic resources for gaining reliable information. Libraries are most appreciated by patients and family members who want lots of information, or very specific information that goes beyond what they find in handouts and the open internet. Most libraries have books, booklets, and audio-visual selections on a wide variety of health topics, and they usually offer online access to special sites. Some libraries also hold classes for patients on such topics as finding reliable information on the internet.

Libraries are usually staffed by professional librarians and other information specialists who can help patients find the information they seek. Major medical centers usually have a patient library for those seeking high levels of health care information. Libraries are sometimes referred to as **knowledge centers**. Some are set up for both professionals and patients and others are designed mainly for patients and their families.

Learning Centers – Learning centers can be another name for libraries, or they can be something different. Basically, learning centers can be anything you plan them to be, as long as they help patients learn in one way or another. Some of these centers are highly specialized for certain types of patients, others offer extensive information on many topics, and others offer only limited information such as pamphlets and booklets. Some are staffed by librarians and/or other information specialists and some are staffed by volunteers. If your medical center does not have the resources for a library, you may consider setting up a learning center to give patients additional learning options.

Helpful features – Both libraries and learning centers should consider offering most of the following features:

- Current and older books on a wide variety of topics related to the health issues of patients at your medical center. In addition to medical topics, offer books on supportive topics such as nutrition, coping, dealing with emotions, and good ways to communicate with health care professionals and loved ones.
- Medical journals – Since most journals are now available online, it's not necessary to have the hard copies in a patient library or learning center, but create awareness about them and how to access them online.
- Computers that offer free access to special patient and professional sites that are not generally available without subscription fees.
- A printer and a photocopier.
- Study tables and chairs.
- Some lounge chairs for relaxation and learning.
- Video selections that they can watch at the center or take home as a DVD's.
- Staff who can help patients find the information they seek.
- Bulletin boards with rotating displays of information on important topics.

Medical Charts, Diagrams, and Models
Best for Helping Patients Understand During Consultations

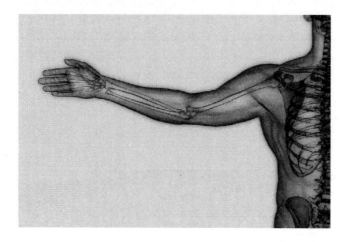

Add to consult rooms – Every consultation room should be set up with visual aids. Health care providers should use them to help patients understand their health problems and treatments better. These charts, diagrams, and models increase the understanding of patients and family members since they encourage learning by both hearing and seeing.

Good options – There are several types of visual aids:
- Laminated wall charts
- Electronic charts, diagrams, and animations shown on a screen
- Hand-held models, generally made of plastic and available from medical education suppliers
- Printed diagrams – These diagrams are sometimes available as sheets in a pad that health care providers can tear off and use for each patient. These printed versions work well because patients can take them home afterwards with markings and notes. You can design and print your own versions of these diagrams for use.
- The educational materials that you give to patients at their consultations may have medical diagrams printed inside, so you can use these to illustrate your explanations.

Develop your own set of illustrated consultation handouts – Patients may find it very helpful if you develop a special handout sheet to support consultations. They can take these sheets home as a clarification and summary of the discussion. Keep them brief and clear. Consider including the following features on these consultation sheets:

- Simple diagram of the body, or part of the body related to specific health issues of the patients you see. If only one part of the body is featured, show how that part fits with the rest of the body. These illustrations can be simple line drawings. If you make them too detailed or complex, they may confuse rather than clarify. Health care providers can draw on these illustrations to help patients understand their specific issues.
- Include blank lines for care providers to write down the names of specific health problems so patients are clear about their issues. Many patients tend to be confused about what is actually wrong with them.
- If it seems like a good idea for your practice, also leave some space on the sheet to identify the planned treatments and/or to briefly show the process of care they can expect.
- These sheets are a good place to include contact information and emergency information for patient reference.

Bulletin Boards
Best for Creating Awareness

The role of bulletin boards – Even though bulletin boards are very basic ways to inform patients, and even though technology offers better options, there is still a place for these boards. However, what you offer on bulletin boards should be viewed as supplementary to more direct ways of informing and educating patients. There are different types of boards to consider using, including traditional cork, and slicker plastic, metal, and glass versions.

Types of information to post – Here are the types of information that work well on bulletin boards:

117

- Promotion for patient learning events, including month-at-a-glance schedules
- Promotion of helpful patient support services
- Announcements of anything of relevance to patients
- Ideas and inspiration
- Posters about supportive organizations
- Education features clarifying health issues
- Reports on current and promising research

Bulletin board guidelines – Manage bulletin boards well so they don't become messy with overlapping and outdated posters. These messy boards look bad and are generally ignored because chaos increases stress. Here are some suggestions to keep bulletin boards organized and current:

- Hang bulletin boards in strategic places where patients will see them, but not be dominated by them. Don't clutter every wall with these boards or with extra notices. If there are posters everywhere, patients will tend to tune them all out since they seem overwhelming. Give them a few key focal points.
- Make sure the boards themselves are framed attractively and fit into the surrounding décor.
  - If you don't manage the boards yourself, designate somebody to do it well.
  - Establish guidelines in your medical center as to the process of getting posters on the boards. You may be using the boards mainly for patient education, but you may be sharing them with other departments. You can inform staff and outside organizations how all posters need to be submitted in certain ways at certain times for approval and posting. If you are accepting posters from others, let them know the number of bulletin boards in your center so they can submit the right amount of posters.
  - Keep everything current with outdated posters removed and replaced.
  - Don't overlap anything, and arrange every poster neatly in relation to others.
  - Attach all 4 corners of posters to the board. If you don't, they will hang in various ways and look messy.

- Patients and others will try to post things on your boards to promote products or ideas. Watch for these and take them down since they are not approved or appropriate.
- If there is not enough room on the board, then prioritize or rotate the information by selecting what is most interesting and helpful to patients at that time.
- For a big promotional impact, post 3 identical posters side by side, or vertically. When something is repeated in a row, it gets more attention.
- Good poster design is essential for getting attention. If you are designing posters for the board, don't overcrowd the content on posters, make sure the main heading really stands out, and include something that catches attention. Refer to the chapter called *Design Everything Well*.

Information Exhibits and Fairs

Best for Creating Specific Awareness and for Interacting with Patients

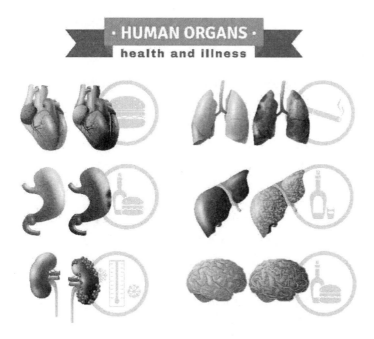

The role of exhibits – Exhibits are any type of educational or promotional displays that you set up to catch the interests of patients and/or the public. Most exhibits are temporary, but some can be created for long-term influence. The best ones are staffed, but there is also a role for self-educating exhibits. These are some of the benefits of using exhibits as an educational initiative:

- If they are well positioned and planned, they can catch the attention of many patients and others.
- There is a lot of flexibility in how you set up exhibits and what you display.
- They offer the chance to show and tell. You can show almost anything of significance and explain many concepts and processes.
- They serve well to create awareness, promote patient education programs and materials, and to solicit participation.
- They can show and advocate healthy lifestyle choices and offer information and tools to encourage change.
- When staffed, they offer a great chance to interact with people.
  - o You can gather much information by asking questions about the interests, needs, and opinions of patients who come by.
  - o You can provide them with specific information and support.
  - o You can make helpful contacts.
  - o You may be able to offer related appointments, recommendations, and referrals.

How to set up good exhibits – A table of brochures is a boring and mostly ineffective exhibit. Here are some ways to make them better:

- Determine the purpose of the exhibit and then plan to create the desired impact.
- Use large and clear signage to identify the topic of the display.
- Be creative and use bold color.
- Prepare them to look neat and professional. Cover and drape tables, as in corporate displays.
- Create exhibits to be as interesting and interactive as possible.
  - o Employ friendly, engaging professionals to staff them.
  - o Display more than documents. Show models, videos, equipment, products, and whatever else if appropriate for the topic.
  - o Plan demonstrations of processes, equipment, or products,

when appropriate.

- If the display is mainly for adults, offer practical information and benefits since adults are most interested in things that can help them in real ways.
- Give things away such as documents, cards, pens, product samples, and whatever else people like. What you give away, should be designed to be at least a small reminder of what you want them to remember or think about.
- Look on the internet for even more ideas on how to make displays attractive and impactful.

The role of fairs – Information fairs are a collection of several exhibits set up together to inform and educate. Fairs can be coordinated in various ways for a wide scope of purposes, so there is no standard way to set them up. But hosting several interactive displays together during a selected timeframe can catch the interest of many patients and others. It can work well to create awareness, inform them about important topics or services, and to offer them practical benefits. Fairs can be set up independently or they can be connected to a larger event such as a special presentation or conference.

How to set up fairs – Here are some guidelines for setting up fairs for maximum impact:

- Determine the main purpose of the fair, and then coordinate the best collection of displays to create the intended impact. Most fairs center around a main topic or theme such as *Support for Cancer Patients* or *Healthy Living Choices*.
- Confirm details clearly with all exhibitors ahead of the event. They need to know the exact location, set up and take down times, active display times, and your expectations.
- Encourage those who have exhibits to make them as interesting, attractive, and interactive as possible.
- Arrange the exhibits so there is a good entrance and good flow through them.
- Hold the fairs in places where many patients or the public will see them and come to look. If you hold them in obscure places, very few people will come, even if well promoted, unless the topic is especially compelling.

- Promote the fairs on posters, in newsletters, on digital screens, on your websites, and in whatever ways you reasonably can. But some exhibits and fairs may be set up just for the regular flow of patients or the public through certain areas and may not need special promotion.

How Newsletters Can Help to Educate

Newsletters and other news features help to show patients that your medical center is actively engaged in caring for them. Newsletters can catch the attention of patients and inform them of continual progress in health care. They can also be a forum for promoting education programs and for directly educating them on topics of general interest. Something featured as news can be more compelling and influential with patients than more static education sources.

Your newsletter may be a simple photocopied page, it may be a colorful production with many pages, or it may be electronic and exist only online. Many large medical centers have developed contracts with outside communication agencies that develop and distribute newsletters for the centers. If an outside agency does this work for your center, find out how to connect with this agency to add education pieces to the productions.

Types of Newsletters

Printed versions – These printed newsletters are developed by staff at your medical center, or by an outside agency contracted to develop the production. They are then distributed in various ways such as reception desks, patient packages, pamphlet racks, and mailouts. These printed versions should be developed at least 4 times a year, but every month may be more ideal for major centers.

Online versions – Online versions of the newsletter are featured on your websites, and they can be developed internally or by an outside agency. They may be developed specifically for the websites, or they may be electronic versions of printed copies, if you choose to have both. If your news features are only on your websites, they can be updated at any time. People will expect more frequent updates on websites than with printed versions since your sites should seem active.

Digital information screens – Digital information screens in busy patient areas are an excellent way to feature news and education features. Most of these screens have a loop of circulating information, so find ways to work with the programmers to insert key information for patients within these loops. Update news frequently, but education pieces can be displayed for longer periods. If you have news features in other sources in addition to these screens, make sure that the information is consistent wherever it is featured.

Social media – Using social media such as Facebook® and Twitter® can be another effective way to inform and educate patients, if you encourage them to connect, and then make the experience worthwhile. Determine what types of news and information patients want to see to keep their interest. Twitter® can be a good way to send out short health facts, updates, and reminders, and a way to promote educational events. Facebook® allows for much more, so you can feature photos, videos, and interactive components. To keep patients engaged, you'll probably need to post something interesting at least once a week.

Ideas for Informative News Features

Here are some topics that work well to help educate in various type of newsletters:
- Information on the benefits of leaning and how patients can influence their care by becoming empowered with knowledge.
- Features on recommended lifestyle habits and how they can benefit patients.
- Features on specific types of self-care to empower patients to be more independent.
- Testimonies and quotations of patients talking about their health. challenges and learning experiences in a positive way. These patient features can be done in text or video.
- Doctors and other professionals explaining key concepts or revealing insight to help patients understand health care more

clearly, either by text or video.
- Ongoing series of articles or videos on a range of related health topics.
- News about the positive effects of patient education programs and how they have helped empower patients at your medical center.
- News about new education options for patients and families.

Steps for Developing
Programs and Resources

Be a Champion to Make It Happen

For any real change or improvement in educating patients, you or somebody at your medical center needs to become the champion to make it happen. Somebody needs to care enough, to recognize the urgent needs, to believe in the many benefits, and to commit to improving care by empowering patients with essential knowledge. It may be a doctor or nurse who works with patients, sees the gaps and decides that something needs to be done. This champion may be a manager who recognizes the need and leads out in the hiring of a Patient Education Specialist. Or it may be somebody who is already a patient educator and determines to take the programs and materials to the next level. The champion can arise out of a wide range of current roles, but one needs to come forth and initiate the changes, whether this person is the one to actually make the changes or not.

You may work at a small medical office where you can lead out by using the suggestions in this book to start educating patients better right away. But if you work in a large medical center, you will need to convince managers and other health care providers that improving patient education is very important. Since each center is unique, there is no standard formula for the champion to use. Here are a few suggestions on how a designated or self-appointed champion may be able to help initiate a process of change and improvement:

- Identify current gaps in patient education in a general way, with some specific examples.
    - You don't need to do an assessment at this point, but you are most likely aware of the gaps and problems in the current situation.
    - Stories are powerful since they affect the emotions as well as the intellect, so think of a case or two where patients have had a negative experience because of lack of information. Relate these cases along with your rational arguments.
- List the benefits of improved education for both patients and the medical center, including higher patient satisfaction, improved outcomes, created efficiencies, and possible cost savings.
- Present some ideas in a brief preliminary plan on what can be done to educate patients better and how to possibly make it

happen.

- Use this book as a reference for specific information and ideas to help in persuasion, including the chapters that list and describe the many benefits of educating patients well.
- Show a passion and commitment to helping make things better for the sake of patients and the center.

Look at the Big Picture

To educate patients well, you will make the biggest impact if you approach it systematically rather than in random bits and pieces. A random approach where you hand out a few pamphlets and draw rough illustrations on the protective paper of exams tables will have little benefit. Instead, identify the real needs and address them in a planned and organized way to make a big difference. Even if you can only begin meeting the needs in small increments, each of these pieces becomes part of the big picture that grows clearer with each new development.

How to Assess the Needs

Once you have support to move forward with changes and improvements, the first step to educating your patients better is to clearly assess the needs. These needs are the current gaps and problems in effectively educating your patients. Look at the whole initiative as a problem-solution type of situation. Determine the problems, the ways that patients are not currently being educated well. Then you'll be able to work on developing solutions to solve these problems. The better you perceive the needs and the more closely you develop programs and materials to meet these needs, the more your patients and center will benefit. Education is integral to good care, so a lack of effective education is a serious breach of care.

There are many ways to assess needs such as questionnaires, interviews, focus groups, consultations, and various types of research projects. Assessments focus on getting opinions from staff, from patients, from professional educators and administrators, and some from all of the above. No type of assessment will give you a full perspective because they are all limited in their scope and biased by such factors as the types of questions posed. Most patients don't actually know what types of education they want or need. However, almost any type of assessment will gather valuable information to help guide your initiative, so do what you can as quickly as you can.

A simple, quick, and fairly objective approach to assessing the needs will probably work best for you. This assessment, as presented below, may be carried out effectively by a manager, educator, doctor, or nurse within a department or a small practice. If you work at a large medical center, work collaboratively with key front-line care providers and others to gain the broad insight you seek.

Basic Needs Assessment for Patient Education

1. List each type of patient
- Identify each type of patient that you deal with and name each one. For example, you can identify them by such names as *Testicular Cancer Patients* or *New Diabetes Patients.*
- You can group similar types of patients together.
- If you work at a large medical center with a full range of patients, you may want to start off by dealing with some priority groups of patients, and then assess other groups at a later time.

2. Identify each major intervention

- Under the names for each main type of patient, now list the main intervention appointments they will most likely experience.
- Number the interventions in order.
- Identify each main type of intervention appointment. For example, you can identify them by calling them such names as *1st Consultation, Hysterectomy Surgery*, and *Radiation Treatments*.
- Group identical types of interventions together under one heading. For example, if this type of patient will be coming back for 7 physiotherapy sessions, group and number them all together by saying *Interventions 5 to 12 – Physiotherapy Sessions*.

3. Rate the education now provided at each intervention

- Since most main medical interventions should include effective education, under each intervention indicate how much education is now provided. To get an accurate assessment, ask several staff members and patients for specifics on what is offered verbally and what materials and other types of supportive education are currently provided. Use these 3 indicators:
  o **No Education** – No education currently provided
  o **Limited Education** – Little or poor education now provided
  o **Good Education** – Effective education now provided

4. Indicate the problems or benefits of the current situation

- Now, under each of the indicators (*No Education, Limited Education*, or *Good Education*) briefly describe the current **problems** or **benefits** of the current situation.
  o For example, if no education is provided at certain key interventions, indicate what problems are now apparent or probable because of the lack of good education.
  o If good education is now provided, list the benefits that are apparent or probable.

5. Propose a solution to the current gaps and problems

- Finally, for the interventions where *No Education* or *Limited*

Education is now provided, type the word **Solution** and under it briefly list the topics that should be covered at these interventions to fill in the education gaps that now exist.

  o Basically, patients should understand their medical problems, tests, surgeries, and treatments each step of the way so their minds are in sync with their bodies.

  o For now, just outline the major topic areas on which patients need to be educated. When you work to meet the needs, you can get more details and decide on how to best meet them.

- You may want to refer to other chapters in this book for help in filling out and reporting your assessment. You will find chapters on what patients need to know and the benefits of education. You may also find it helpful to look at standards and information from other organizations involved in supporting and educating the types of patients you deal with.

6. Develop a summarizing report

- Now you have an assessment for each type of identified patient, their main interventions, the education currently provided, and outlines of solutions to the current gaps.

- Compile the results into a document to show key stakeholders and use as a basis for moving forward. If you work at a small center, just highlight the problems and solutions on the assessment pages. But if you work at a large center, consider compiling the information into a clear report about the current gaps, along with strong recommendations and preliminary plans for addressing them. See the suggestions in the next chapter about preparing a report that goes beyond just summarizing the assessment results.

Here is an example of an assessment that emphasizes problems resulting from a lack of effective education. This example is quite detailed, but don't feel that you need to offer so much detail. You can create much briefer versions as long as you use key words that clarify the problems and solutions. Or you may choose to create even more detailed versions if you want to create a comprehensive report to convince stakeholders of the needs.

Day-Surgery Patients – Assessment of Education Problems with Proposed Solutions

Intervention #1 – Patients visits doctor with medical problems and are scheduled for tests to help with diagnosis

- **No Education**
  - Since problem has not been diagnosed, no need for any medical education at this point.
- **Solution**
  - New patients should receive a printed or electronic patient guide to the medical center since they will be coming back for tests and possible surgery and need practical information on the facility.

Intervention #2 – Patients arrive to have scheduled tests

- **Limited Education** – patients have only received an appointment schedule for their tests.
  - Since patients have little or no idea what the tests will involve they are confused and stressed about the tests.
  - Since specific preparation was necessary for some of the tests, patients are now coming unprepared, so some tests need to be rescheduled because of lack of clear information. This rescheduling causes inefficiencies in departments and extra costs for the center.
- **Solution**
  - Whoever schedules tests for patients needs to give them clear printed or electronic information:
    - Name and description of each test they will have
    - The purpose of each test
    - The location and timeframe of each test
    - Specific preparation instructions for each test
    - Specific instructions for after the tests, if any, such as needing somebody to accompany them home

Intervention #3 – Patients return to doctor who identifies their problems and schedules minor surgeries to resolve them

- **Limited Education** – *doctor just names the problems and states that they will be scheduled for surgeries to resolve them.*
  - *Since the problems have only been verbally identified, patients sometimes don't remember the correct name of their problems, and they don't know much or anything about their upcoming surgeries.*
  - *Patients tend to be confused and stressed about their problems and about the upcoming day surgeries because they don't really know what's going to happen.*
  - *Patients start looking on the internet for insight, even though they don't know what information applies to them. This confusion and distress affects the patients negatively, makes them tense about the surgeries and may result in negative feelings toward their care providers and the medical center since they have not felt important enough to be nurtured with helpful information.*
- **Solution**
  - *When the medical problems and the surgical solutions have been identified, the doctor or assistants need to give patients clear information on:*
    - *The names and nature of their medical problems*
    - *The names, descriptions and explanations of their scheduled surgeries and how they may work to treat their medical problems*
    - *Very specific preparation instructions for their surgeries*
    - *Clear instructions on the date, time, and location of their surgeries*
    - *After surgery instruction, such as when they will probably be discharged, and whether somebody needs to pick them up and take them home afterwards*

Intervention #4 – Patients arrive at the medical center for surgeries

- **No Education** – *patients are given sedation without any explanation about the process of surgery.*

- o *Patients often arrive confused and distressed since they don't know any specifics about the surgeries, and some of them have misinformation.*
- o *If specific preparation was required but not clearly explained and given to them in documents, they may arrive unprepared, so the surgeries may need to be delayed or rescheduled resulting in inefficiencies and extra costs.*
- **Solution** – *same as for intervention #3*

Intervention #5 – Patients are discharged from the medical center after day-surgeries

- **Limited Education** – *nurses offer a few verbal instructions about recovery and tell the patients when to return for post-surgery checkups.*
  - o *Patients are confused and stressed about what has been done to them since the surgeries were never explained to them.*
  - o *Since patients need to provide self-care during the recovery process, they may not remember the verbal instructions from the nurses very well and therefore don't adhere well with recovery requirements. By not following the requirements, many patients are now jeopardizing their recovery. In some cases, serious side effects develop, such as developing blood clots because they did not take their blood thinning medications regularly.*
  - o *Lack of education is causing some patients a slow, poor, or complicated recovery that not only harms them but can greatly harm the medical center by such factors as extra interventions, a poor reputation, and lawsuits.*
- **Solution**
  - o *The discharge nurses need to supplement verbal instructions with printed or electronic instructions for all day-surgery patients with the following information:*
    - ▪ *What patients should expect during the recovery process, including side effects and timeframes*
    - ▪ *Very clear instructions on everything they need to do to recover well from the surgeries, including taking medications and all other types of specific self-care*

- *What symptoms to watch for that may be a reason for concern, and what to do if they appear*
- *Contact information for their health care team in case of any concerns or needed care*

Intervention #6 – Patients return to doctor for post-surgery checkups

- **No Education** – *only brief comments on good recovery or further problems that need addressing.*
  - o *No specific medical education may need to be provided at this point.*
- **Solution**
  - o *Even though no medical information may be necessary at this point, there are possibly some lifestyle recommendations that will help keep patients from developing similar problems in the future. Without this information, patients may develop similar or worse problems later. These recommendations should be verbally expressed by the doctors and supported with printed or electronic information.*

So, now you have done your assessment. It specifically highlights the gaps and problems that exist for each main intervention for each type of patient. With the problems identified, you can now start planning to provide solutions.

Now Develop a Plan to Meet the Needs

If you work in a small medical office or a somewhat autonomous department, you may have very basic goals, such as developing a new brochure for your patients. You may not be trying to change the bigger systems or deal with a broad scope of patients. If so, you may not need to bring a team together to develop a detailed plan. But approach even small projects systematically and proceed toward your goals using the best available expertise and the related ideas in this book.

For major initiatives with a broad scope of patients, you will achieve the most by developing a **written plan** to meet the scope of patient information needs. **Your main goals are clear:**

- **Ensure that effective education is integral to the care of your patients for health, practical, and legal reasons.**
- **Fill in the current learning gaps to address the resulting problems and provide the needed benefits.**
- **Plan the best overall and specific ways to empower your patients with helpful knowledge.**

Work in collaboration with others to develop the plan so you get valuable input from several professionals and patients. At large medical centers, consider forming a special committee or working group for this planning phase. In smaller centers, you may choose to work more informally with a couple of other staff members and a patient or two. Direct and coordinate the interactions to keep things moving forward in a cohesive way. Generally, when staff realize the benefits of educating patients, they are eager to help as much as they can. Develop your plan as concisely as possible, but with enough details to make the points clear.

There is more than one way to develop a plan, so proceed in the way that works best for you and others at your center. But here are some important steps to consider:

1. Name your document

Before you write your plan, think of a good name for the plan so it has a clear identity and helps you visualize the goals. Here are some ideas for names:

- *Problems and Solutions – Plan to Benefit Patients Through Education at Name of Medical Center*
- *Education Strategies to Empower Patients at Name of Medical Center*
- *Patient Education at Name of Medical Center – Proposal to Improve Outcomes and Reduce Costs*
- *Filling in the Information Gaps – Plan to Enhance and Extend Patient Education at Name of Medical Center*
- *The Power of Patient Education – New Initiatives for Name of Medical Center*

2. Summarize the current education gaps and resulting problems

First, present the problems so you can set the stage for the solutions later in the plan. Refer to your assessment of current needs to compile a list of the gaps and the problems that result from them. You may choose to list all of the gaps together and then describe the problems in the next section. Or you may choose to identify each of the main gaps together with brief descriptions of the resulting problems, one after the other.

If you have done assessments of just a few types of patients, then you can be very specific. If you have assessed many types of patients, you may choose to be a bit more general and summarize the main gaps and problems. You can include the detailed assessment reports as an addendum for reference, so you don't need to include every specific detail in your plan.

If you are seeking support and funding for your proposal, make sure to identify and emphasize the existing gaps and resulting problems. You must clearly present the current situation as problematic with an urgent need to be addressed. Doctors and administrators often require compelling documentation to be convinced and supportive.

To strengthen your understanding of the gaps and to create a greater impact with your proposal, look to some outside health care standards that show the types of information your patients should know. Your country probably has several medical organizations that help to regulate and support the care of patients. There are national accrediting organizations such as *The Joint Commission* in the USA, and you will find societies, associations, and foundations around the world for conditions such as cancer, diabetes, heart disease, and arthritis. Show how the gaps in the knowledge of your patients is emphasized by the information and standards presented by these organizations.

3. Now present the planned solutions

Now offer specific solutions to the problems caused by education gaps. This section is the core of your written plan. First you need to decide on the solutions that will work best in your center, with the input from all key stakeholders, including patients. Then you will need to propose those solutions in a clear, organized, and convincing way.

In your assessments, you proposed solutions to each specific problem. Those are important for reference, but in this written plan, develop and present a more comprehensive approach. If you don't plan within the larger framework, then the bits and pieces won't fit together when they are developed and implemented. Just filling the gaps is too narrow an approach. Step back to look at the big picture of patient education so you can plan to fill the gaps within the context of an overall strategy at your center.

In your presentation of solutions, choose an approach that works best for your situation and style. You can propose broad new initiatives that will effectively take care of the specific problems that you listed earlier in the plan. Or you can group certain types of problems together, and then present your plans to address each of those groups of problems.

There is more than one good way to educate patients, so determine your general approach, based on time, expertise, and resources. You may decide on a progressive approach where you implement basic education to begin with and then add other elements, options, or approaches in months and years to come.

Keep in mind that patient education needs to be integrated into the process of medical care at your center. It should not be something added on, but incorporated as a key component of care. Think of how to integrate education realistically and effectively by working with other health care providers as well as patients.

More Ideas for Writing Your Plan:

- First present and describe the **big picture** of your plan and then the details to support it. Decide on your **main** and **supplementary approaches** to meeting the patients' needs, then explain how they will work to address current problems and provide ongoing benefits.
  - o For example, your main approach may be to develop a set of printed materials to hand out during consultations, but your supplementary plan is to also set up some classes to help patients learn even more.

- o Develop a diagram to help clarify your plan with its main and supplementary approaches. A good diagram puts things in perspective for yourself and others.
- Now present the details. Focus on the topics of information that patients really need to learn, then propose one or more effective ways to help the patients learn the essential information. Make sure all of these proposals work together within your comprehensive approach.
- These questions may help you to think of what to propose:
  - o What should patients learn at each intervention?
  - o What do the patients seem to not understand well now?
  - o While referring to the information and standards of outside health organizations, where do our patients fall short in their knowledge?
  - o What main topic areas, or points do we need to help the patients to learn?
  - o What are the priorities?
  - o What are the effective ways to help patients learn this information? What options will work best here?
  - o What is our plan? What do we need to access, adopt, adapt or develop?
  - o What information is for all patients, and what information is for specific type of patients? How do we direct the general education and the specific education?
- Consider the following education options: (all of these options are described in detail in the section of this book called *The Best Ways to Educate*)
  - o Order existing materials from outside sources to give to patients at consultations as a quick way to fill in some gaps.
  - o Order printed or electronic charts for consultation rooms to enhance consultations.
  - o Develop a new set of handouts or brochures to reflect the process of care at your medical center.
  - o Direct patients to a specific section of your website for learning.
  - o Develop new content and better illustrations for your website.
  - o Set up both required and optional classes for patients to attend so they can learn about many topics that doctors and nurses don't have time to teach them.

- Plan patient conferences at regular intervals for specific types of patients that need extra support.
- Plan to develop simple videos and a virtual tour to help your patients learn well visually.

Make Sure Your Plan is SMART:

As you develop your written plan, consider the SMART way to propose solutions. Don't become burdened by these concepts and feel that they are too much to deal with. Just read them through and keep them in mind as you are developing your plan since they will help direct and refine your ideas:

- **S – specific**
  - Be specific enough to be meaningful in the problems you describe and in the solutions that you propose. Plan broad initiatives, but then provide specific details to support them. In this written plan, you don't need to provide all the details for every aspect of the plan, but provide enough for the framework and direction to be clear.
- **M – measurable**
  - If your patients were tested before and after the education you provide, the test results should show that they did learn the essential information. This does not mean that you need to test your patients, but plan your education solutions to offer results that can be measured and confirmed in some way.
- **A – achievable**
  - You may have many brilliant ideas about how to help your patients learn, but make sure that they are achievable with the time and resources available at your center. Developing video productions and new website dimensions may provide dynamic ways for your patients to learn, but they can use a lot of time and funds. Sometimes it's best to start off with some basic education and then enhance it with further developments when they can be achieved. So, keep what is achievable in mind in your proposed solutions.
- **R – realistic**
  - This point is similar to achievable, but in an even broader sense. It basically means to plan within the scope of your real

situation and the real world. If you are part of a big professional medical team with lots of funding, then the scope of your real world is much bigger than if you are a nurse working alone to make things better. Dreaming has its place, but don't lose your grip on reality.

- **T – timely**
  - o Plan to educate your patients as well as you can, as soon as you can. But keep a good balance between quality and speed. Don't just grab and present the closest brochures available to fill in a gap if they are not well developed. But don't get so bogged down in planning and developing learning options that they rarely get implemented. Plan to offer basic solutions first, and then more comprehensive solutions within a reasonable timeframe.[6]

4. Project the costs

- For each part of the plan, determine the resources you will need and estimate the costs as well as you can.
- Summarize the costs for different parts of the plan, and then the total costs at the end.
- You may propose more than one plan to address the needs and show the costs for each. Developing a simple pamphlet will cost much less than a major media production.
- Also indicate whether the projects are funded, or if you are making a request for funding.
  - o If you are making a request for funding, make a note about possible cost savings for the medical center resulting from such factors as efficiencies created by the education initiatives.
  - o Refer to the chapter here entitled *How to Access Funding*.

5. Name the staff who are involved or will be involved

Include names or positions of the staff who are involved, will be involved, or may be involved in these patient education initiatives.

---

[6] Doran, G.T. (1981). There is a S.M.A.R.T. way to write management's goals and objectives. *Management Review*, 70(11), 35-36

- Clarify the roles of each professional involved. This way the expertise needed for the development and implementation procedures is identified and assigned.
- If you need to get more staff involved, then explain whether they would need to be hired, or contracted, and at what cost. Also clarify whether you can access the expertise of those already on staff, with permission, for certain roles in the plan, such as teaching a class.

6. Include a timeline for developments and implementation

Assuming you will get support for your plan, provide a reasonable timeline for the development and implementation for each main part of your initiative. Timelines show that you have thought through the details of making it happen. For those who may provide support, timelines also make the whole plan seem more real and help them to visualize actual changes in patient care at your center.

7. Highlight the benefits of empowering patients with knowledge

If you need to convince others that your plan is worthwhile, end with a section highlighting the benefits of empowering patients with knowledge, both for them and for the medical center. Refer to the chapters in *The Power of Patient Education* section near the beginning of this book.

8. Submit your plan for approval and support

Finally, present the plan to the managers and administrators who can potentially approve and support the proposed initiatives.

If you have the opportunity, present your plan in a compelling way to stakeholders, managers, and administrators. Develop impactful electronic slides. Order your points from current problems to proposed solutions with real benefits in the future. If keen professionals and patients worked with you to develop the plan, consider co-presenting with them to add viewpoints and dimensions.

Ideally, your managers and administrators will find the plan convincing and they will respond by approving, supporting, and funding your initiatives. If you don't get that affirmation, don't give up on finding ways to educate patients. There may be delays and challenges, but steadily make small improvements that will add up to big benefits over time.

If you are a manager or administrator, you may have the power and influence to take this initiative forward right away for the benefit of patients and your medical center.

Who Are the Patient Educators?

Almost all health care providers are also patient educators. Educating minds goes along with treating bodies, but some care providers recognize and fill this role better than others. When health professionals realize the powerful effects of empowering patients with knowledge, they tend to want to do it better. This book is written as a practical guide to help care providers find ways to educate more effectively.

Education should be integrated into the process of care for all patients. It should not be viewed as separate or supplementary, but integral to quality care. When the minds of patients are in sync with what is happening with their bodies, a whole new dimension of enhanced care becomes possible because of their understanding and participation.

In major medical centers, educating patients requires a whole team of health care providers to teach patients at key times during the process of their care. In small centers, one or two professionals

143

may do all of the educating during consultations and at other times and ways.

For patient education initiatives to be most effective, they need to be centrally coordinated. Especially at larger medical centers, somebody needs to fill the role of **Patient Education Specialist**. This role may be a part time role for somebody such as a nurse, or it may be a full time role for a professional with both a medical and an education background. It may be a realignment of current staff, or it may be somebody newly hired to take on this position. The more time and interest this person has for this role, the better the resulting education. The Patient Education Specialist is the central coordinator and supporter of the education activities by other professionals. But the Specialist should also be very active in planning, developing, and implementing programs and resources for strategic use. The Specialist may also do much of the educating directly, such as teaching classes for patients.

Patient Education Specialist Qualifications

- Have an interest and passion for educating patients well.
- Understand patients and their real needs.
- Have a health care or an education degree along with health education experience.
- Be committed to evidence-based education.
- Be committed to clear communication.
- Have the ability to plan, develop, implement, and manage a whole range of learning options for patients.
- Have the ability to lead out in the development of many types of education initiatives including writing, teaching, website developments, and video and media productions.
- Have the ability to work well with all types of medical professionals to create awareness of education initiatives and to gain their support and participation.
- Be willing and able to connect with the surrounding community and outside professionals to gain support and to find opportunities for collaboration that will benefit patient learning.
- Have the ability to collaborate with other professionals to find effective ways to empower patients with essential knowledge.
- Be willing and able to assess and evaluate patient needs, as well as the effectiveness of the learning options implemented.
- Be willing to work hard, keep learning, overcome barriers, and collaborate well to steadily improve patient education options and effectiveness.

The Extended Education Team

In addition to the Patient Education Specialist, there are many other professionals who should be involved in the education process to ensure it is well integrated into health care. Some of these people will educate patients directly, and others will be involved in the development of programs, materials, websites, and videos. You will have some of these educators on staff, and others you may choose to hire as consultants for specific projects:

- Doctors
- Physicians' Assistants
- Nurses and Nurse Practitioners
- Therapists
- Information Specialists (librarians)
- Dietitians
- Exercise Specialists
- Complementary Therapy Specialists
- Social Workers
- Psychologists
- Spiritual Care Specialists
- Researchers
- Presenters
- Writers and editors
- Website managers and developers
- Photographers
- Video and media specialists
- Graphic designers, illustrators, photographers
- Materials managers and distributors

Also Let Patients Educate Other Patients

Patients are good at educating other patients, so help them find roles and then coach them. Here are some ways to use patients in the process:

- **Stories** – At patient classes and conferences, or on videos, arrange for patients to talk about their own experiences in dealing with health problems and treatments. They add real life perspectives that other patients can identify with and be encouraged by. Carefully select and coach participants. These patient testimonies (stories) add a personal and emotional component to education sessions, and they tend to be very well received by other patients in attendance. The medical presentations by professionals should be balanced by real patient stories.
- **Word of mouth** – Patients tend to talk with each other socially in waiting areas. When they have been educated well, they will spread what they know, and they will also promote the learning

options that they find helpful. This exchange of insight, ideas, and recommendations can raise awareness and add clarity.

- **Features** – Materials and websites can be enhanced by features or quotations from patients who have already experienced care from you or others at the medical center. These features of real patients create interest and understanding for current patients.

- **Q and A** – At live or web-connected learning sessions, always plan time for discussions. Patients learn from each other and identify with each other as various patients ask questions and get answers. In their questions, patients often reveal something about their own experience that offers insight for other patients in attendance.

- **Program and resource development** – Invite current or former patients to get involved in planning, developing and evaluating programs and materials. Their perspectives are very valuable and may determine whether an initiative is effective or not in meeting real patient needs. But you will need to balance the personal opinions of your patients with professional input.

When to Use Existing Sources of Information and When to Develop Your Own

Determine what your patients need to know, and then find out what already exists to help your patients learn the information well. If appropriate materials, programs, websites, and videos already exist, and they are available to you, then use them. If nothing appropriate exists, or if access is restricted, then find a way to develop your own. In some cases, you can use a combination of existing information and your own developments to reach certain objectives.

There are many sources of health information that you may want to access and use, or direct your patients to find:

- **Local, national, and international support organizations** – Supportive, charitable organizations have been established for almost every type of health problem, especially for major diseases. These organizations include cancer societies, diabetes associations, heart and stroke foundations, and other special support agencies. Many of these organizations have produced valuable educational materials that you can order to use for your patients, usually at no cost. Most of them also have extensive websites that you can direct your patients to find.

- **Drug companies** – Pharmaceutical companies produce materials, websites, and videos on health issues and treatments. Some of this information is promotional and not appropriate for educating patients objectively. But they produce two types of information that patients find very helpful:
  - One, they offer very specific information for patients who have been prescribed to take their drugs. These sheets, brochures, or web links offer patients insight and instructions to help them gain the most benefits from the drugs while minimizing and managing side effects.
  - Also, drug companies sometimes produce very objective, evidence-based health information brochures, booklets, and web links as a "public service". These sources of information are usually well produced and available to order for your patients at no cost.
- **Government departments and agencies** – Since governments want to enhance the health of citizens, they offer information and support such as pamphlets, websites, and resources on many topics. In addition to your own local and national government options, check out what other governments and agencies offer too.
- **Health education companies** – Consider looking into what health education companies offer for your patients. They produce very helpful materials, websites, charts, models, videos, and products that you can order for use at your center. These companies are businesses, so there are costs, but they are usually reasonable, and they often offer discounts for ordering multiple copies.
  - For example, *Krames®* is a US education company that offers a wide range of materials and products. Even if you don't work in the USA, you should be able to order through a partnering agent in your country.
  - There are other medical education companies that develop

content for websites. They sell you the content that you can then personalize and use on your website. Just make sure the content reflects the care that you offer.

- **Information developed by other medical centers** – Other medical centers across your country and around the world have developed extensive information on nearly every health topic. If you search for specific types of information, you will most likely find something that closely suits your needs. But you cannot take information from any other source without giving credit to the developers. With written permission, you may be able to adopt or adapt this information to help educate your patients. If you find something very useful, contact the developers to see if they will give you permission to use their content in one way or another. You can also direct patients to their sites, if appropriate.

Checklist for Using Outside Sources of Information

If you choose to use existing information sources, use this checklist to determine whether they are appropriate. You will probably not find any information sources that are perfect in every way, but check to make sure the following characteristics reach an acceptable standard. The information should be:

Appropriate for your education goals
- ☐ Objective and evidence-based
- ☐ Unbiased
- ☐ Accurate
- ☐ Current

- ☐ Easy to read, listen to, or watch (at appropriate reading/learning level)
- ☐ Well designed and organized with a good flow
- ☐ Well illustrated, where appropriate
- ☐ Available to you at no cost, or a cost you can afford

Some printed materials are able to be personalized with the name and logo of your medical center. But don't dismiss good sources of information just because you can't personalize them. You can find other ways to personalize information such as putting a pamphlet from an outside source inside a folder that features the name and logo of your center.

Reasons for Developing Your Own Information

Even though there are many outside sources of well-produced health care information, you will most likely find a need to develop some of your own materials, website features, and videos to represent the specific care that you provide. Plan to produce your own educational information when you have a need or desire to:

- Develop learning options that are of a higher quality or more suited to your learning objectives than anything you have found from outside sources.
- Develop or enhance your patient guide and/or website with information that fully orients patients to your medical office, department, or medical center.
- Promote, distinguish, and brand the special care and treatment options offered by your office, department, or medical center.
- Emphasize the unique qualities, services, expertise, processes and reputation of your care.
- Personalize the information with specific descriptions and photos of your facilities, your departments, your process of care, and your staff.
- Instruct patients in very specific ways about the surgeries, treatments, procedures, and process of care they will experience at your center.
- Develop a unique set of materials that will work together as a special set and also reflect your programs, website, and media learning options.
- Develop information that clearly instructs patients on specific self-care procedures, processes, or lifestyle changes. This type of information can empower them to partner with you in several aspects of health care such as managing conditions or recovering from surgery.
- Create awareness of a whole new medical initiative, treatment, trial or approach to care offered at your office, department, or medical center.

Steps to Developing Your Own Educational Content

A Quick and Simple Approach

Sometimes, developing new information for documents or your website can be a quick and simple process:

- Type out the new content, or get the right expert to provide it.
- Check to make sure the information is –
  - Written in clear, plain language
  - Current and accurate
  - Illustrated with at least simple sketches or photos, if helpful
- Get approval from whoever else needs to be involved.
- Organize the information to look good on the page.
- Print and photocopy the new information sheet to give patients.
- Or, update your website with the new information.

This basic approach may sometimes be appropriate for new handouts or quick updates, but for most professional developments, follow the steps outlined below.

When you need to develop educational content for documents, your website, or other purposes, take the necessary steps to ensure the clarity and quality of the information. You can develop content in various ways, but here is an approach to consider:

Steps for Major Developments

Select a team of experts (if needed) – You may be working independently in a small medical office or department, and you may have many abilities yourself, so you may not need a whole team of experts. But the bigger your work facility, and the more patients and professionals you work with, the more need for a team approach. Some experts are other health care providers who commit to helping part time, or you can hire outside consultants for certain tasks. If you are planning significant developments, you will need the following experts, at least part of the time:

- Project coordinator
- Content experts (doctors, nurses, therapists, researchers, or others)
- Writers
- Editors
- Graphic designers
- Illustrators
- Photographers
- Printers
- Web developers
- Media specialists, if developing videos or other special media productions

(1)   Identify a specific need to address – You most likely see many patient needs for more and better information. When patients are confused, uncompliant, or misdirected, there are probably corresponding gaps. You may have identified others through an assessment, such as the one described earlier in this book. Since you can't meet all the needs at once, take on the challenges one at a time. Identify a priority need and then work to address it. But it does help to have a bigger plan so you see how all developments will work together to meet the needs of your patients.

(2)   Clarify the need – Clarification is necessary so you really know the scope and characteristics of each development. Get clarification from both the professionals and the patients involved in this area of care.

- What types of patients need this information?
- What information do these patients need? What are the topic areas that need to be covered?
- How will the information benefit these patients? What are the objectives of writing this content?
- How much detail is necessary?
- What are the best ways to make this information clear and practical?
- What format or formats will help the patients learn this information best – handout, pamphlet, booklet, website feature, video?

(3)   Check what information is already available – Check both internally and externally to see what already exists, if you have not done this already. There is no use working hard to develop new content when it has already been written well by somebody else. If something is available, can it be *adopted* or *adapted* to meet your objectives? If so, you may have little or no work to do, but don't copy somebody else's content if you don't have permission. Often, what is available is not exactly what you need, but it can be helpful as a reference when developing your own.

(4)   Get the new information you need – You may not need to do much or any research to write for some projects, because you already know the content or have easy reference to it. But when you need to find information, there are many reference sources that you can use. Don't get bogged down in doing more research than is reasonable for each project, but make sure to do enough so you are aware of the scope and current facts. Always give appropriate credit to your sources.

- **Content experts** – The nature of the content determines who the content experts are, so seek out the ones you need. The most likely experts are the internal health care professionals with whom you work.
- **Professional journals** – Offer ideas and insight into health care as well as extensive research results for almost every type of care.

- **Libraries** – Medical libraries provide search assistance and access to many specialized sources of information.
- **Books** – While books may not have the latest information about developments, they offer extensive information about most topics.
- **Internet** – The internet offers an almost limitless supply of ideas and information on almost every topic, but make sure the sources are reliable.
- **Internal research** – Connect with the researchers at your medical center to find out what they have discovered about specific health issues and treatments, or consider doing new research.
- **Interviews and focus groups** – Conduct them with various experts and with patients and family members to gain insight and personal perspectives.
- **Drug information** – Pharmaceutical companies provide detailed information on the drugs they produce, and independent research reveals the effects of these drugs.
- **Websites and publications from other institutions** – Check out what other institutions have written and produced about your featured topics. While you cannot plagiarize or use their content without permission, it can give you ideas on the types of information to include and options for organizing your content.

(5)   Connect with your internal content experts –You may be the expert for some types of content. Doctors, nurses, therapists, and researchers are usually the content experts for health care information. If you are coordinating the project, and if you are not the content expert yourself, meet with the key internal content experts. Even if you are the expert, connect with others in your department to get their input as well.

Discuss the need specifically and decide how to best get the content necessary for the project. Sometimes doctors or nurses will consent to dictating or typing the basic information for you, or they may direct you to good sources where you can glean the content. Make decisions and get commitments about getting the core information within certain timeframes. Clarify what role you will play and what roles others will play in the project.

(6)   Write the new information into a patient-friendly document – Bring together all of the information you need for the project from content experts and other sources. Now write it into a patient-friendly document that will be the basis of a new publication, a website addition, a teaching session, or a video. Organize the document into sections with headings and subheadings, and use paragraph breaks and bullet points where appropriate. Also make sure the language is simple and that it flows well for easy understanding. Refer to the chapter in this book entitled *Be Very Clear – Plain Language Guidelines.* If you are not doing this yourself, direct this part of the development to a writer who is willing and able to take the information and make it readable for patients.

(7)   Get input from professionals and patients – When you have written the new information for patients, get input from key professionals who may be using this information to educate. It's a good idea to get input into this content before you develop it further into a pamphlet, web feature, or whatever you have planned. It's much easier to make changes to the basic document than trying to do it after further developments.

Also get patient input before you finalize the information to make sure they find it easy to understand and practical to use. You can approach a few patients in waiting areas to give you input, or you can set up more formal patient reviewers. These patient reviewers can be current or former patients who are keen to be involved. They may be willing to volunteer their time, or you may offer them some compensation. You don't have to implement everything recommended by patients since they each have their own perspectives and opinions, but take their input seriously as you balance it with a professional perspective.

(8)   Illustrate, design, and format the information – Once you have refined the content and received approval from stakeholders, then illustrate and design the information for its intended purpose. It may be just a simple printed sheet that you develop in Word ®, or it may be a full color booklet, a website feature, or the script for a new video. Some information does not need to be illustrated, but visuals help the learning process in most cases. You may be doing the design and layout yourself, or you may have other design and production specialists involved. Refer to the chapters in this book called *Show as Well as Tell – The Importance of Visual Learning* and *Design Everything Well* to ensure high standards.

If you are working with others, keep them at least somewhat involved in the design and illustration process if they need to approve of the ultimate production.

(9)   Include a disclaimer – To protect both patients and the medical center from misunderstandings and legal problems, include a disclaimer on all your materials, videos, and website. Basically say that *"This information is not intended to replace the direct care and instructions of your health care providers."*

(10)   Confirm with the checklist – In the end, your new information source should have the following characteristics:

□ Evidence-based, accurate, and current
□ Reflects the practice and policies of your office, department, and/or medical center
□ Meets the objectives by addressing the patient information needs
□ Well-organized, designed and illustrated
□ Written in plain language, flows well, and is easy to understand
□ Has input from patients and approval from key stakeholders

(11)   Print or produce the new information – If you have prepared a document for printing, now get it printed for distribution to your patients. If you have written information for your website, add it along with illustrations. If you have prepared content for a new or updated teaching session, then create slides to go with the notes. If you have written the script for a video, get it produced. There is no use developing new information unless it gets to your patients, so provide the content to them in the most accessible ways. The new information you have prepared can most likely be used in more than one way.

(12)   Evaluate usage and refine as needed – When the new information has been introduced into the process of care, evaluate its effectiveness in helping patients learn. Evaluate formally if you have the time and resources, or informally until you can do it more comprehensively. If you are not conducting a detailed evaluation at this time, talk with care providers to get their observations and opinions about effectiveness. Also talk with a few patients to ask them some directed questions on how helpful they find the information. Take notes during your discussions. You can learn a lot in a short time through these casual chats that help to confirm that the information is working well, or if some changes are necessary. If indicated, make changes or refinements as soon as possible.

How to Access Funding

Patient education is integral to health care. As a health care provider, you have an obligation to educate patients about the nature of their conditions, their surgery and treatment options, their preparations and recoveries, their medications, and their self-care procedures. While some types of education may be optional, providing patients with core information is not, and you have practical, medical, and legal responsibilities to offer it clearly and well.

157

It takes funding to educate patients effectively, but well-directed investments will result in better care, increased self-care, process efficiencies, improved outcomes, and reduced costs. Here are some possible sources of funding:

Request Core Funding

If you are part of the management team at your medical center, work with other team members to direct funding into patient education initiatives since it is essential to quality care. If you are not part of the management team, request funding from the team at your medical center. Clearly present the current situation and needs, explain the practical and legal obligations, list the benefits of enhancing education, and present your plan with the projected costs. You need to present a strong case and show passion and commitment to making it happen. See the chapter called *Now Develop a Plan to Meet the Needs* for more details.

Appeal to Health Charities, Foundations, and Fundraisers

There are charities, foundations, and fundraisers connected with many types of health problems and with most large medical centers. They generally raise money and direct it to specific projects they see as significant and helpful for patients. Present your plan and request funding from these organizations since they exist to help worthy causes and meet real needs. To get their attention, make your requests specific, and show how you plan to meet the real needs of people who are disadvantaged now. They may be willing to sponsor such things as the development of new programs and materials, an educational event, or a learning center. You may need to work with the management team of your center to help make your request formal.

Apply for Research Grants

Apply for research grants to fund certain types of patient education initiatives. Plan the initiatives strategically with supporting details showing how the initiatives work to benefit patients in measurable ways. You will probably need to collaborate with clinical care providers to make these initiatives workable. If you collect data showing how the initiatives benefit patients, there is a good chance of getting regular funding for the initiatives after the study has ended. Also consider research initiatives that show how patient education benefits medical centers by creating efficiencies and saving time and money.

Appeal to Corporations for Funding

There are many companies who are willing to offer generous donations to projects at medical centers, as long as they are acknowledged in some clear way. Of course, this type of support offers them promotion, positive media reports, and tax deductions, so it is not completely altruistic. Most likely your center has policies regarding such donations to prevent any bias in medical care. At some centers, these corporations are required to donate through foundations rather than directly to a project. Check out the policies and procedures at your center to see what options you have for accessing this type of support.

If you are allowed, directly ask for the support of selected companies for specific initiatives. Work with management to catch the interest and response of these companies. These corporations like to be seen as meeting real needs and associated with the human interest stories of those who benefit from what they offer.

Some companies look for good opportunities to sponsor a cause. If you are already doing impressive work in patient education, you may be fortunate enough to catch the attention of corporate leaders who will approach you and ask how they can help. If your office, department, or center provides exceptional care, corporations want to be associated with the success and may willingly offer funding.

Inspire Individual Donors

There are philanthropists in every country who look for ways to spend their money for the benefit of others. When these people become aware of an urgent need, they may ask how they can donate to a project or initiative to meet the need. If these people have been cared for at your medical center, or if they have had family members cared for impressively, they may be inspired to contribute to the center to help ensure a high standard of care. If you are ever approached, be prepared to discuss your work and projects to further encourage them to offer support. Your center has policies regarding such donations, so regard them carefully. Since these donors will want a receipt to use for tax purposes, they will most likely donate through a medical foundation associated with your center.

Collaborate with Other Organizations

There are organizations in every country that offer support to people dealing with specific health problems. For example, many countries have cancer societies that offer information and supportive services to those dealing with cancer. You are probably aware of many of these organizations already. They raise funds to support people dealing with health problems, even though they don't usually offer direct medical care. Since your center does offer treatments to some or all of these types of patients, the support organizations may be very happy to collaborate with you. They may want to be involved in programs, patient conferences, or other initiatives. They may be looking for ways to have more access to these patients and to provide supplementary help beyond what your center offers. So, connect with the leaders of these organizations to discuss ways you may work together to help patients learn. Besides offering you helpful materials to give patients at no cost, they may pay some or all of the expenses of events and initiatives.

Charge Patients for Participation

If your center allows, and if there seems to be no other way to cover some costs, charge patients a reasonable fee to participate in events such as classes, special presentations, and patient conferences. If you promote the sessions well, and if you offer great learning options with practical value, patients and family member will be willing to pay. In some cases, you may choose to only charge for certain things such as refreshments or materials.

Raise Funds

If allowed, plan and implement creative ways to raise funds for patient education initiatives, if you cannot get funding in other ways. Here are some possibilities:

- **Organize a small or large fundraising campaign or event** – If you are planning a large campaign or event, work with professional fundraisers to help ensure it is effective. To get participation, appeal to emotions with human interest stories of how patients will benefit.
- **Sell special items** – Create or access items to sell on a short or long term basis. The traditional "bake sale" may not be appropriate, but there are many things people will buy to support a good cause. Work with a promotions company to manufacture unique items to sell, with or without a logo and message. Arrange for somebody to create unique jewellery or ornaments to sell at a gift shop, or at a special sale. Solicit people to donate artwork to sell at an art show at your center. Make sure that whatever you sell has value to the buyers.
- **Partner with retail** – Certain retail chains help institutions raise funds in various ways. They may set up donations boxes, or they may sell certain products for a period of time with the profits donated to good causes. They may directly ask for small donations when customers make regular purchases. This type of fundraising is variable and evolving, but it can be an effective way to get funding if you have a good plan and make the right connections.
- **Try crowdfunding** – There are ways for new companies to get funded by making compelling requests over the internet. People in need have often been funded by presenting their situation on social media. This is a variable and evolving way to raise funds that requires a creative strategy as well as business and legal consultation. But explore this possibility if you have run out of other funding options.

Evaluate Programs, Materials, and Patient Learning

You may feel that you are so busy trying to get information to patients in one way or another that you don't have time for evaluation, or you may feel you have no ability or interest in evaluating programs and materials. However, there are several good reasons to evaluate the learning options offered to your patients:

- Helps you know if patients find the various programs and materials understandable and helpful.
- Helps you know what patients like and don't like.
- Helps you know what information patients are actually learning.
- Helps you know how each education initiative is contributing to the care of your patients.
- Helps you know how to enhance learning options to educate patients better.
- Gives you increasing insight into how to educate your patients effectively.
- Gives you data to support the work you are doing, which can be the basis for more funding and more staff. You can also use the data as content for professional publications and presentations.

In an ideal world, large medical centers would have a team of patient educators with one of them focused on research and evaluation to support all of the learning initiatives. If that is not your reality, then find a way to conduct simple evaluations. You can develop a one page questionnaire and give it to a representative number of patients to fill out. If you can arrange the time, fill out the questionnaires yourself as you briefly interview patients. Patients generally don't like filling out forms, but most are very happy to talk with you and answer your questions as you record their responses. Other advantages of interviewing them include the ability to interact, make clarifications, point out specifics, and get more insightful responses.

Evaluation is most helpful during these times:

- Just before you finalize programs, materials, or other new developments
- A few weeks after you implement new education initiatives to see how well they are working
- Before updates or revisions to any of the sources of information that you offer
- Whenever there is a reason to question the effectiveness of the education you currently offer

Some Ways to Evaluate

There are many ways to evaluate. The more time, expertise, and resources you have, the more strategic and comprehensive your evaluations can be. Here are some approaches you can take:

- **Simple questionnaire** – Develop a simple set of questions on your computer and hand it to patients or interview them for responses. Form most questions with easy response selections such as *yes* or *no*, multiple choice, or on a scale of 1 to 10. This makes it easy for patients to fill them out and for you to calculate responses. But also consider including a few open questions where patients can provide longer responses that offer insight into some key areas.
- **More complex questionnaires** –Testing specialists develop sophisticated and comprehensive questionnaires for various purposes. You'll find these specialists at universities, and they can help you develop questionnaires able to be read and analyzed by computers. This type of evaluation has the advantage of electronic assistance, but the disadvantage of being limited to multiple choice questions, so you don't get insightful comments this way. If you are trying to figure out exactly how much knowledge patients have about certain topics, then these sophisticated questionnaires can be a good way to test them. But many patients do find these types of questionnaires confusing since they have to make marks in certain places in specific ways on a grid-like sheet.
- **Online surveys** – You can develop online questionnaires for patients, put them on your website and then direct patients to them. Or you can use online services, such as *SurveyMonkey*

®, to give you some interesting and effective ways to evaluate what you are doing for patients. Some patients will not be comfortable responding to such surveys, but they are a helpful way to get some patients to evaluate your efforts to educate them.

- **Focus groups** – While setting up a focus group with selected patients does require some planning and coordination, once you have them all together, they generally offer very valuable insight into the learning options you offer. Keep them on topic so you get the input you seek, pay for their parking, and compensate them with an honorarium for coming.

- **Staff input** – To find out if patients are really learning what they need to know, discuss learning with other care providers who deal with these patients. These front line professionals can let you know the effects of education initiatives and give suggestions for a better approach if current programs and materials are not effective. Plan exactly what you need to ask them to gain the insight you need, rather than chatting randomly.

These questions may help you gain the insight that you need. There is more than one way to ask these questions, but here are some key queries:

Important Questions for Evaluations

- Did you understand what you read, heard, or watched?
- Are there any parts you did not understand? If so, what parts?
- Were you able to follow the information from point to point? If not, what was confusing and how can we make easier to understand?
- What are the most important things that you learned that you did not know before?
- What parts did you find most helpful?
- How is this information going to help you?
- Are you now able to follow the instructions and perform this procedure (or whatever) on your own?
- What did you like best about _____?
- Are there any parts that you did not like? If so, what parts and why?
- Did the illustrations (slides, video, or whatever visuals were used) help you to understand the information more clearly?
- Do you like the way the pamphlet (or booklet, or program, or whatever is being evaluated) looks? Do you have any suggestions on how we can make it look better?
- What can we do to make the pamphlet (or booklet, or program, or whatever format) better so it would help you more?
- What topics (or information) were missing that you think we should have included?
- Does this information help you to understand that you need to call about a problem you may experience? If so, what is that problem?
- Does this information let you know how you can manage a problem at home without needing to call? If so, what is that problem and how will you manage it?
- Would you have preferred to learn this information in another way? If so, what way?

Questions for Classes, Presentations, Webinars, and some Videos:

- Did you find this session interesting and helpful? If so, what information did you find most interesting and helpful?
- Were you able to understand the speaker clearly? If not, why not?
- Were the slides easy to follow and understand? If not, what was confusing?
- Did the presenter give you enough time to ask questions and make comments?
- Did you learn anything from the other patients who made comments or asked questions during the discussion? If so, what is one thing that you learned?
- Are you now able to follow the instructions and perform this procedure (or whatever) on your own?
- What did you like most about the session?
- Is there anything that you did not like about the session? If so, what and why?
- What can we do to make the session better next time we offer it?

What Do Patients Really Need to Know?

How to Determine Patient Information Needs

Generally, the more care that patients need, the more education you should offer them.

If patients have common or minor medical problems with quick or familiar resolutions, they may not need much educating. But you should still offer these patients clear explanations and concise printed materials or media links to information. What may seem routine or minor to you as a health care provider, may seem like a big deal to them.

The patients who will benefit most from being well educated are those dealing with serious health issues that require:

- Extensive tests, exams, and procedures for diagnosis
- Major surgery
- Major or extended treatments
- One or more types of therapy
- Continual medical care and self-care for chronic problems
- Continual monitoring of status and changes for those with unstable health
- Help to adjust to a changed life after surviving a major health crisis
- Changes in lifestyle habits to manage, control, or resolve health issues caused by their poor choices
- Help to deal with new disabilities and limitations
- Multi-dimensional support for palliative care

In most cases, the basic process of education involves two main parts:

ONE: Verbally educate patients
- Can be in consultations or group sessions
- Use visuals to increase understanding and retention
- Allow time for discussion

TWO: Then give them printed or electronic information for reference and further learning

There are many ways to educate effectively, as you will see in the chapters in this book on *The Best Ways to Educate*, so use the approaches that work best for you and your patients.

What do these patients really need to know? Below, you will find detailed sections outlining the main information that will benefit patients within most types of health care interventions:

The Framework of Essential Knowledge

Appointment Clarification and Confirmation

Who needs to know?
Patients who are being scheduled for new appointments of any type.

Almost all outpatient health care, and much inpatient care, happens at scheduled appointments between patients and health care providers. These appointments are set up for a full range purposes, interactions, and interventions. Scheduling appropriate appointments and ensuring that patients have the correct information is of utmost importance to facilitate care. Whoever manages bookings needs to clarify and confirm the following essential information to patients for each appointment. A verbal confirmation is not enough. All verbal bookings should be further confirmed and supported with specific printed or electronic information.

What they need to know:

- Exact time and date
- Clear directions on where to go
    o Map, transportation options, and parking instructions
- The purpose of the appointment
- Who (type of health care provider) they will see at the appointment
- List of what to bring or not to bring
- Pre and post-appointment instructions, if any
- Approximate length of the appointment
- Costs and payment information, if any
- Contact information for the booking office

Medical Center Information

Who needs to know?
Patients who will be receiving a major medical intervention or a series of treatments at a medical center.

Most health care providers work at medical centers, so patients should have the chance to learn about the center. Offering patients key information about medical centers is mostly a matter of creating awareness rather than an educational process, but it is essential for practical navigation purposes. Give patients a printed or electronic version of a **Patient Guide** on or before their first visit.

What they need to know:

- The name of the medical center
- The location of the medical center
  - Location map and clear directions
  - Transportation options, including parking instructions
- Key navigation information
  - The location of all departments and services related to their care
  - The location of support services and amenities and how to access them
  - Campus maps and facility floorplans
- Contact information for all departments and services
- Patient rights, responsibilities, and opportunities
- The medical center's responsibilities and commitment to patients
- Financial information on costs, payments, and insurance, if any
- Important facts about the medical center that may or may not include the following:
  - Local, national or international significance
  - Special expertise, services, and technology
  - Interesting or promotional statistics
  - History
  - Affiliations
  - Patient-centered approach to care
  - Donor support

o Significance of the center's name, such as connection to a person, group, concept, or specialty

Health Problem Information

Who needs to know?
All patients with health problems.

Present this information to patients when they are first diagnosed. This knowledge is most important for patients who will have an intense intervention or extended process of care for serious health issues.

What they need to know:

- The names of their health problems
- The nature of their health problems, described and explained
- The location of the problems, if location specific
- The causes of the problems
- The effects of the problems
- If they have more than one medical problem, an understanding of how their problems relate to each other, if associated
- The general prognoses of their medical problems
- (Surgery and treatment information included in other sections)

Test and Exam Preparation

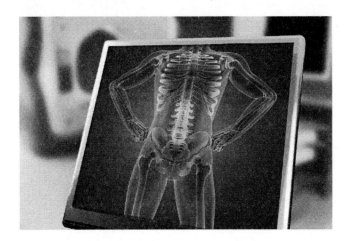

Who needs to know?
All patients who are scheduled for tests or exams, especially major ones such as MRI's, PET scans, and heart endurance tests. Present it to them as soon as they are scheduled.

What they need to know:

- The name of the tests and exams scheduled for them
- The purpose of the tests and exams
- General timeframe for the tests and exams
- Preparation instructions for each test and exam, if any
- Costs and payment information, if any
- Post-test and exam instructions, if any
    - For example, the need to arrange for somebody to drive them home because of sedation
- Indication of who will discuss the results of the tests and exams with them

Informed Consent Information and Documents

Who needs to know?
Patients who have a choice of more than one surgical or treatment option.

For patients who have a choice, make sure to empower them to make the choice. Educate them on their options, letting them know the surgical or treatment processes and the benefits and risks of each option in comparison to the others. Then provide an informed consent form for the option they choose.

What they need to know:

- Clear details about each surgical or treatment option. If possible, present each of their options in a similar way so they can see them "side-by-side" for comparison
  - The names and descriptions of all of their viable options
  - An overview of the process and experience of each option
  - The possible benefits and risks of each option
  - The costs of each option, if any
- Treatment recommendations by their primary care provider, along with the reasons for this recommendation
  - Offer them time for discussion and clarification
  - If they have a choice, make sure they know the recommendation does not nullify their ability to choose
- Medical and legal details for informed consent
- Clarification of legal issues related to informed consent
- Informed consent documents to read and sign

Possible approaches:
For patients who have important but non-urgent decisions to make, consider offering them clarify in the following ways:

- Printed materials or website links to comparative information about their treatment options
- Extra discussion time with experts
- Moderated discussion time with former patients who have chosen various treatment options
- Special group sessions where experts present and discuss the treatment options in comparison to each other. Possibly arrange to have experts from each of the options present their perspectives and invite open discussion at the end of the presentations. This approach has been helpful for prostate cancer patients who commonly have several treatment options.

Surgery and Treatment Preparation

Who needs to know?
All patients who are preparing for major interventions such as surgeries, treatments, or a series of treatments.

As discussed above, if they have treatment decisions to make, they should receive this information with time for consideration to help them make informed choices.

What they need to know:

- The surgical and treatment options available for their medical problems
- Identification of the specific surgery or treatments scheduled for each of them
  - Include main reasons why this surgery or these treatments were chosen over other options, if they had a choice
- How these surgeries or treatments may work to resolve their problems – simple scientific explanations
- The objectives of their personal surgery or treatments (goals of care)
- The possible side effects of their surgeries or treatments
  - Include what they and the health care team can do to address these possible effects
- The process of these surgeries or these treatments – what they will most likely experience
- The roles of health care providers during these interventions
  - Such as who will perform the surgeries or offer the treatments
  - Contact information for their health care teams
- Their specific role in the surgeries or treatments
  - Instructions for how to prepare
  - Instructions for their roles during the interventions, if any
  - Instructions for what to expect and how to respond during immediate recovery, such as waking after surgery
  - Instructions for the assistance of family members or others

A possible approach:

Group preparation classes tend to work well to help prepare some types of patients who will be undergoing surgeries or treatments. For example, a class on preparing for chemotherapy can be an efficient and effective way to provide an overview for some cancer patients, but they also need individual instruction on their specific drugs and possible side effects.

Surgery and Treatment Recovery

Who needs to know?

Patients who have just had surgeries, treatments, or a series of treatments. Close family members and personal care providers may need to know this information as well so they can assist the patients.

In some cases, patients and their helpers need to have this information before they undergo the interventions so they know what to expect and how to participate.

What they need to know:

- Clear information on what was done and what was achieved, or not done or achieved, during the surgeries or treatments
- The process of recovery – what they will most likely experience
- Their specific role in the recovery process
  - Instructions on what, when and how to perform all types of self-care

- How to monitor their recovery, and what indicators require attention if they arise
- Instructions for the assistance of family members or others
- The roles of health care providers during their recovery
  - Contact information for their health care teams
- Next steps in their care, if other interventions are suggested or planned
- Instructions and recommendations for long term recovery and for achieving and maintaining the best health possible

Prescription Drug Information and Instructions

Who needs to know?
All patients who are prescribed drugs to take on their own.

Instruct them verbally when they receive their first prescription, and offer them printed or electronic insight and instructions as well.

What they need to know:

- The names of each of their prescribed drugs
- The general role of each of these drugs
  - The desired effect of these drugs
  - How the drugs work in the body to achieve these effects – basic explanation
- Clear instructions for taking the drugs
  - Exact dosage of each drug

- o Times to take each drug
- o When to begin and when to stop taking each drug
- Drug and food interactions to avoid
- The possible side effects of each of these drugs
  - o What the health care team can do to address these possible effects
  - o What they can do to address these possible effects
- Contact information for their health care teams

Hospital Admission Orientation

Who needs to know?
All patients being admitted as inpatients to a hospital or other type of medical center.

This information helps them feel welcome and provides them with an awareness of care and comfort options.

What they need to know:

- The layout of their units, including locations such as nursing stations, visiting areas, and entry and exit points
- Room information and instructions for such things as washroom usage, bed position controls, the call button, and visitor guidelines
- For those who are able to move around, hospital services such as supportive departments, the chapel, eating places, lounge areas, gardens, events, and amenities
- Overview of what they can expect during the process of their care during their stay
- Specific patient instructions for them, such as rules, expectations, schedules, mealtimes, and appointments
- Any information that is helpful for family members and others who will be around the hospital visiting and caring for the patient

Possible approaches:

- Ideally, welcome each new patient, give them a brief verbal orientation, and then give them a hospital guide. If the information guide is on their TV or online, encourage them to view it. Since some patients are admitted during emergencies, find a way to provide them with information, if and when they are able to appreciate it.

- Offering a live orientation session about care at the medical center can be very helpful for patients entering a process of care as outpatients for such problems as diabetes and cancer. You can also provide orientations on your website or with videos, but there are many benefits to a live session. See the chapter here called *Patient Classes and Other Sessions* for details about orientations.

Self-Care Training

Who needs to know?
Patients who are being empowered to provide some of their own care.

A great deal of health care is now provided by patients and family members, when they are trained and directed by their health care providers. This self-care enables patients to play an active role, and it can reduce dependency on professionals and reduce costs for medical centers. There are hundreds of activities and procedures that patients can be trained to do for themselves, including:

- Taking prescription drugs
  o Patients have long been instructed about taking their

medications at certain times. While most are very capable of this simple version of self-care, many seem to be confused or tend to not comply, so clearer instructions and better training are necessary.

- Performing self-monitoring tests and recording data
- Giving themselves injections
- Changing dressings
- Connecting and disconnecting medication pumps
- Responding to allergy or breathing emergencies
- First aid or emergency care for themselves or others
- Performing physical exercises and therapies

What they need to know:

- On what days, timeframes, and situations they should perform these procedures
- A list of everything they will need to perform the procedures
  - How to get what they need, if not provided directly
  - Instructions for preparing and laying out the items, if appropriate
- Step by step instructions of exactly what they need to do
  - Use numbers to indicate the progression of each step
  - If a family member or another assistant will be involved in performing the procedures, then offer clear directions for the roles of everyone who will be participating
- Why these self-care procedures are important for their care
- Who to contact for help, if they have problems performing the procedures

Training tips:
Some types of self-care require more instruction than others, and different patients learn in different ways, so there is no exact formula to the process. Be as attentive and comprehensive as you need to be in each situation. Here are some guidelines for training:

1) Offer clear verbal instructions with a demonstration of the procedures, either individually or to groups of patients.
2) Give patients the time to ask questions, practice the procedures, and then demonstrate their competence. For the

most critical procedures, patients definitely should show their competence before attempting it at home.

3) Give patients illustrated instruction documents to take home for reference. Some basic instructions may not require illustrations, but they are essential for most procedures with critical steps. Simple line drawings can work well.

4) In some cases, offering an instruction DVD or a link to an online video can play a helpful role for training and reference. You may want to encourage patients or family members to video instructions and demonstrations on their smart phones for reference at home.

Lifestyle Modification Recommendations

Who needs to know?
Patients who have medical problems that were likely caused or affected by poor lifestyle choices.

What they need to know:

- Specific lifestyle habits that are problematic
- How these specific lifestyle habits may cause and affect their medical problems
- What specific changes are strongly recommended
- Guidelines for making these changes
- How these lifestyle changes may help manage, control, or resolve their medical problems
- The benefits of adhering and the possible consequences of not adhering to the advice
- Key sources of help to make these changes, in the medical center and in the community, and how to access them

Possible approaches:

- Some of these patients can be difficult to educate since they may be resistant or feel helpless to change their lifestyle habits. They may be resistant to learn and not open to change, even if they realize that they should.
- For much more insight, refer to the chapter here called *How to*

Get Patients to Participate in Their Care and Make Lifestyle Changes.

Connections to Specific Types of Support

Who needs to know?
Patients who need or may want support for their medical issues, beyond what you can provide.

Some health issues are quickly resolved and patients are able to go on with their lives without much disruption. But many health issues require major interventions, long periods of unresolved waiting, extended treatments and recoveries, or ongoing chronic care. Many patients dealing with these health problems over a long period of time will benefit from supportive connections that address the issues they face. Since you will not be able to provide all of the support, offer these patients information and recommendations and/or referrals to other sources of support. You can develop short reference directories to give patients, or make individual recommendations.

What they need to know:

- Services in the medical center such as counselling, spiritual care, nutrition, fitness, and various therapies
- Local, national, and international organizations that offer information and support for people dealing with their types of health conditions. Most of these organizations have charitable funding so their services are generally free.
- Government programs, services, and agencies that offer support for health issues
- Sources of financial help
- Face to face support groups
- Online chat and support groups
- 12 step programs
- Businesses that offer specific products and services to benefit patients
- Community organizations and drop-in centers set up to help people deal with various issues

- Books that are very relevant to patient challenges
- Websites that offer reliable information and support

Survivorship Strategies

Who needs to know?
All survivors of life-threatening health issues.

There are different definitions of what *survivor* means, but most agree that the term refers to a person who is still alive after encountering life threatening health problems. Dealing with such a health crisis changes people in many respects. It often changes their bodies, their abilities, their families, and their futures. These people need help to survive and to live as well as possible, even if the health crisis has passed.

What they need to know:
Each type of survivor needs information relevant to their issues, but here are the common types of information that benefit these people most:

- How to achieve and maintain their best health
  o Guidelines for eating well
  o Guidelines for being physically active
  o Guidelines for resting and sleeping well
  o Help to overcome addictions, if any
  o Help to make lifestyle changes
  o How to monitor health and when to seek medical attention
- Help to deal with physical challenges –
  o Losses and changes to their bodies
  o Disabilities
  o Late and long term side effects
  o Fatigue
  o Pain
  o Incontinence
  o Sexual functioning
  o Neuropathy
- Help to deal with mental and emotional issues –
  o Stress and fears

- o Sadness or depression
- o Coping with uncertainty
- o Cognitive issues, such as difficulties with memory and concentration
- o Connecting and communicating well with others
- o Sexual functioning issues
- o How to get counselling, therapies, and other professional support
- o How to find peer support, both face-to-face and online
- Help with practical issues –
- o Living arrangements
- o Finances
- o Getting back to work
- o Travelling
- Help to find meaning and make spiritual connections
- How to establish a new "normal" and live as well as possible

Possible approaches:

- One of the best ways to educate these patients is to offer educational sessions where doctors, support professionals, and other survivors provide insight and advice on how to move forward and live their best lives.
- Also provide them with relevant printed materials, electronic links, and references to services for specific types of support.

Palliative Care Information and Support

Who needs to know?
Patients who will not survive their health problems, as well as their families.

Unfortunately, the most advanced medical care cannot save everybody from their health problems, and everybody eventually malfunctions with age. Some people die suddenly, but most die over an extended period of time. Palliative care offers information, direct help, and support for those who are dying and for their loved ones. Ideally, palliative patients begin receiving this type of care many months, or even a few years, before they pass away so they can gain the most benefits. Education of both patients and families is essential to create awareness of the care options and also to help them all deal with the dying process as well as possible.

What they need to know:
Palliative patients and families need information that relates to their individual situations, but here are the common types of information that benefit them most:

- The meaning and benefits of palliative care for patients and families
- Insight to dispel the myths about palliative care and dying
- Help to prevent and deal with physical issues –
  o Disabilities

- o Pain
- o Fatigue
- o Constipation
- o Dehydration
- o Wound care
- o Lack of appetite and weigh loss
- o Swallowing problems
- o Sleep problems
- o Breathing problems
- Help to prevent and deal with cognitive and emotional issues –
  - o Anxiety, stress and distress
  - o Depression
  - o Dementia
  - o Guilt and regret
  - o Grief
- Connection and communication between patients, families, and friends –
  - o Family communication
  - o How to talk with someone who is dying
  - o Forgiveness and reconciliation
  - o Talking with children about death
  - o Family gatherings and rituals
  - o How to say goodbye
  - o How to deal with moments just before and just after death
- Education and help for caregivers –
  - o Making sure to care for one's self
  - o Dealing with medications
  - o How to safely move immobile patients
  - o How to help with eating
  - o How to provide mouth care
  - o How to care for the hair and faces of patients
  - o How to help with bathing
  - o How to help with toileting
  - o How to prevent pressure sores
- How to deal with practical issues and make decisions –
  - o Preparing wills
  - o Preparing financial documents
  - o Preparing health care directives
  - o Deciding where to die, if there are options

- o Planning and preparing for dying at home
- o Planning a funeral
- o Financial assistance and benefits for patients and caregivers
- Help to find meaning and guidance for dying well
  - o Telling, writing, or recording life stories
  - o Finding spiritual meaning and making connections
  - o Living every day as fully as possible
  - o Creating more memories while still alive
  - o Commemorating lives in positive and memorable ways

How to Deal with the Challenges of Educating

Low Literacy

You will encounter many patients who have a limited ability to read and to comprehend the learning options you provide. Some of the most challenged are older patients with failing perceptions and people who don't read and write the common language well. Here are a few things you can do to help those with low literacy learn essential information:

- **Use simple language** – Speak and write using short words within mostly short sentences. See the chapter on simple language called *Be Very Clear – Plain Language Guidelines.*
- **Use illustrations and photos** – Use visuals to supplement your consultations, printed materials, website, and teaching sessions. Illustrations and photos tend to catch patient interest and to visually show and clarify the concepts.
- **Explain more concepts verbally** – People with low literacy tend to understand spoken language better than printed information, so spend a bit more time consulting with them to help them understand. You can use visuals, models, props, gestures and such things to make your points even clearer.
- **Let family members help** – Family members with a better ability to understand often accompany those whose ability is limited. When possible, include these family members in all education efforts since they may comprehend better and then help patients to understand as well. This involvement also encourages family members to be more active in caring for the patients.

Dementia and Other Learning Limitations

Some patients have dementia, brain injuries, or other learning limitations. These limitations can hinder them from absorbing the information from the education options that you offer. Each situation is unique, and there is no general strategy to employ in these challenging cases. Your medical center may have policies and procedures developed that will guide you in the best way to address information needs with these patients. Here are a few suggestions that may help:

- **Speak directly to these patients** – Never ignore patients with learning limitations and assume there is no use in addressing them. Speak with them directly showing that you recognize their value and human dignity. Many of them will understand and benefit from instruction, and even if they don't understand or remember much, they may be able to emotionally connect with the care you show to them.
- **Find out what they can learn and can do** – By talking with these patients and family members, find out what abilities they have. People with dementia are usually quite functional for years, and many patients with brain injuries still have some strong mental abilities. When you understand better what they can comprehend, you will know how to instruct them better. Many of these patients will feel empowered by the challenge of learning and by using that knowledge.
- **Get family members involved** – Family members and other caregivers need to be taught the essential information for these patients with learning limitations. Find out the relationship of these people to the patients so you know their roles in helping the patients. Ensure they are getting the necessary information, even if you are directly addressing the patients.

In addition to cognitive barriers to learning, you will encounter patients who have vision and hearing barriers. They all need special help to get the information they need. If you spend time with them, find out how they function and help them learn within the scope of their active senses. If they can't see, help them learn by hearing. If they can't hear, help them learn by seeing. Always show attentiveness, patience, kindness, and respect.

Multiple Languages

Many countries have become multicultural, so you will likely be dealing with patients who speak other languages and do not know your common language well. At your medical center, you are probably very busy providing education in one language and don't have a way to educate in multiple languages. No matter what your budget, there is no way to provide all of your educational initiatives in multiple languages. Here are some suggestions on how to deal with patients of various language groups:

- **Offer the main education options in a 2nd language** – If you live in a place where a 2nd language group is prominent, do what you can to provide your core materials and other learning options in that language as well as the main language. Most likely there will be staff members who use this other common language, so work with them to translate documents and website information and to teach sessions in the 2nd language.
- **Use a professional interpretation service** – In some countries, you have access to instantaneous language interpretation over the telephone or internet, for a fee. Find out what is available to you at your medical center, along with the costs, so you know how you can best use this service. This professional interpretation service is especially valuable for important consultations and for helping patients to give informed consent for specific surgeries and treatments.

- **Use live interpreters** – Some large medical centers and health systems have interpreters available to book for consultations. These specially trained health care interpreters are ideal, when they are available. When they are not available, family members may be able to help. Patients who don't speak the common language may bring a family member or somebody else with them who does speak the common language. In these cases, speak to both the patients and the interpreters in short phrases and sentences, and then wait for them to pass on the message. Unfortunately, you may not be sure that the information has been passed on accurately since the family member may not understand the terms or concepts well. In addition, family interpreters may intentionally change the message if they don't want patients to know everything. Your medical center may have policies and procedures for live interpretation to help ensure the right messages are getting through.
- **Get your website translated** – When possible, work with internal staff to translate the main content of your website. Otherwise consider using professional programs or hired translators. There are some electronic programs that do this automatically for you, but the resulting translation may not be accurate or clear. Whatever service you use, get the right professionals to review it and make necessary corrections and refinements before launching it to your patients
- **Create links to the best online information in other languages** – Whether you translate your website or not, direct your patients to reliable websites in other languages where they can learn more about their medical conditions and treatment options. Consult with professionals who can help you to find the websites that best reflect your care and treatments. Librarians may be able to help. Once selected, find ways to direct patients to the sites that will help them most.

Lack of Staff and Space

You may be very motivated to enhance patient education at your medical center, but you wonder how to make the changes since you are already lacking staff and space. Or, you may have worked in education for many years and have become discouraged at the slow progress because of lack of resources. If so, you are in a common situation experienced by educators around the world. But you can still help initiate helpful changes if you are passionate and persistent. Here are a few suggestions that may work at your center:

Integrate education into current roles – If you can't hire more staff to work as patient educators, find ways to get current staff more involved:

- Help enhance current consultations by providing visual aids such as charts, models, or computer animations into the consult rooms for the front line care providers to use.
- Meet with doctors, nurses, and other front line professionals to find out what would be most helpful to give out to patients as supplements to their consultations. If possible, access these resources for them, or let them know how to get them. You may consider providing materials for receptionists or clerks to hand out to all patients or selected groups of patients. Handing documents out does not require much extra effort on their part.
- Arrange for qualified internal experts to teach group sessions once a month or so. Usually they are willing and able to help in this way for an hour or two a month. If you line up several of these professionals, you can offer a whole range of classes to patients without any extra hires.
- Connect with the leading health care providers to get their input into the development and use of learning options. Once they are engaged and see the benefits of patient education, they are more likely to want to be involved and will find ways to help enhance learning.
- Request specific help from key professionals for selected learning options, such as asking them to translate a pamphlet into another language. Even in a busy medical center, you can usually find ways to get small bits of help from many people, and all of these bits add up to a large amount of assistance without any extra hires.
- Staff in certain roles may be obligated to help you with education if you approach them about adding education to the areas under their influence. For example, you probably already have internal

or external website professionals who update your websites. They will likely be willing to add and update educational content for you. If your center produces a printed or electronic newsletter, you can find ways to work with the producers to include educational content.

- The more people who are focused on patient education, the more can be accomplished to benefit both patients and the medical center. When possible, work with managers and administrators to show them the specific benefits of patient education and request the staff and resources needed to extend and enhance learning options.

Determine space requirements – You need spaces to educate patients, so determine what spaces you need for each planned option, and then find and use the best available spaces. These are some of the spaces commonly needed:

- An auditorium and classrooms for big and small teaching sessions and special presentations.
- Space to store and organize printed materials for distribution.
- Spaces to display both promotional information and a selection of materials for patients to take.
- Spaces for a patient learning center or centers where they can access computers, books, and media selections. These spaces may be a library, or part of a library, or they can also be one or more special learning centers for certain types of patients.

Influence construction or renovation – If you can, influence any current or future construction plans to include more spaces for patient education.

Find niches in current space – If you can't find or create good learning spaces, find ways to maximize current spaces in your medical center. Here are a few suggestions:

- In most centers, there are various small rooms that were originally constructed for such purposes as janitor supplies, equipment, and consultations. But some of these rooms may be underused and available for new purposes. You have probably walked by some doors that are always closed and you have no idea what's inside. Connect with a building manager and ask for help to find a room or rooms that you might be able to use.

- Since front line professionals, receptionists, and clerks should be giving printed materials to patients, find space in cabinets, shelves and drawers to store these materials. The closer they are to consultation areas, the more likely they will be given to patients.
- In most large medical centers, there is an auditorium and classrooms that may be used primarily by staff and medical students. Find out the current usage schedule of these teaching areas and do your best to reserve time for patient teaching sessions and special presentations. These rooms may be in a nearby building but still available for you to reserve.
- All health care centers have patient waiting areas. These waiting areas can be turned into classrooms after regular clinic hours, and sometimes even during clinic hours. They already have chairs and may have a media screen that can work for presentation slides. At designated times, arrange the chairs so the space works well for group learning sessions. Schedule and promote these sessions as options for patients.
- Patient learning centers should generally be set up in visible areas where most patients pass by regularly. If you can't set up one main space for learning, then try to spread the learning options out by putting a few racks, shelves, and computers in selected waiting areas. Even if you have a main learning center, you may choose to have some smaller ones as well, if you have the funding and resources to set up and manage them.

Dealing with Patients for a Long Time or Short Time

Some medical centers offer comprehensive care with a well-integrated approach, so patients come for the entire scope of their care. In these types of centers, you have both the opportunities and the challenges of dealing with such a broad spectrum of care. You can influence patients more, but you are also more responsible to help them learn the full range of essential information. You can find ways to empower all of these patients, but that requires a lot of work, a bigger team of educators, more resources, and strong administrative support. Make the most of developing and implementing learning options that will help the most patients in the most ways, such as patient guides, websites, and virtual tours, as these establish a framework of understanding for the majority of your patients. Then work to fill in that framework with specific information for all types of patients.

Other medical centers only deal with some types of patients for selected interventions within the broad scope of their care. In these centers, you will only be able to deal with each of the patients for short periods of time. The disadvantage is that you cannot have as much influence on educating and empowering them on their path to health. But the advantage is that you can have a powerful influence on these patients by providing very effective education when you do engage with them. Another advantage is that you have a lot less educating to deliver, so you can focus on fewer productions and fewer types of interventions. In these situations, when you are planning, developing and implementing learning options for patients, look at the full scope of their care both outside and inside your center. By seeing the process broadly and objectively, you will know better how to prepare your education to meet their real information needs. You may choose to provide extra information to help them within this broader scope, as well as provide exceptional education to go along with the portion of care that you offer to them.

In all efforts to educate, keep the whole care process in mind for each type of patient you deal with, whether you are part of that whole process or not. You don't have to educate for the parts you don't deal with, but you will tend to make your education more effective if you present it as part of their bigger story rather than an isolated visit. When you do have a chance to educate these patients, provide them with an impressive learning experience that will help them through the rest of their care, whether it is at your center or not.

Practical Issues – Such as Mobility, Accessibility, and Parking

There are some practical issues that can affect the ways you choose to educate your patients. These issues include such factors as patient mobility, parking problems, and city size. To offer the best education options, you will want your patients to come to the medical center for teaching sessions, in addition to their medical appointments. For patients to respond and come, you need to convince them that the value of these experiences makes coming worthwhile.

Ideally, your patients are mobile, the city is not too big to get around, and parking is close and inexpensive. Many medical centers have these advantages which allow you to educate patients at more times and in more ways. However, some other centers are in big, congested cities where getting around is more challenging. If parking is complicated, crowded and expensive, patients will hesitate to come more than they need to. If your groups of patients have mobility or cognitive issues, then do not even try to get them to come more than absolutely necessary.

So, when you are developing your learning initiatives, keep these practical issues in mind. If there are lots of hassles for patients to come to the medical center, then do your best to schedule group learning sessions at times when these patients will be present for other types of appointments. For some groups of patients, you may be able to incorporate learning sessions right into the flow of their medical care, either before or after consultations or treatments. It's a good idea to offer patients more than one way to learn anyway so they can select to learn in the ways they prefer. Upload videos of learning sessions on your website for patients to access at any time, but remember that patients tend not to watch recorded sessions that are longer than 20 minutes. Setting up webinars can be effective since they are live and interactive, and patients will stay tuned into live sessions longer than recorded sessions. Choose compelling topics and promote them well to get participation.

Make the best plans for education based on many factors, including practical issues. Over time, you will learn what works well and what doesn't, so you can strategically direct and refine the ways that are most effective in educating your patients.

Disagreements about How to Educate

Various professionals have differing ideas on what information should be taught and how it should be taught to patients. These disagreements can become issues that hinder the development and implementation of education initiatives. In these cases, work with management and the content and education experts to find ways to get agreement in a timely way. It may work best to designate one of the lead professionals to make the final call on what information should be presented, but this expert should be fair and diplomatic in considering the scope of views. Another option is to go with the vote of the majority in a designated group or committee. Whenever possible, use evidence from internal and external sources to help determine what education to offer and how to offer it.

In addition to deciding what information to present, you also need to decide how to present it. Take the following considerations to help decide on what approach to take:

- The insight of education specialists on the process of learning
- Patient preferences
- Preference of front line professionals
- Time, resources, and costs
- Best way or ways to integrate education into the current process of care
- The way or ways that that are most accessible or most easily developed and implemented
- Evaluation and research indicators
- Objective evidence from internal and external sources

A Note to Patients

Patients are often the ones who encourage, inspire, and generate change in medical centers, so don't hesitate to help make the practical advice of this book become a reality. All health care providers are also patients at some points in their lives, so their patient experiences should help them to understand your patient perspective and want to ensure you receive effective education.

You are the ones who have needs that must be met, challenges to address, and a life you want to live beyond medical care. You are the ones with bodies, brains, emotions and spirits that need understanding, support, nurturing, and health. You are the ones who connect with your care providers to seek full healing. You are the ones who can call for improvements when you experience gaps in your care and declare that you will not be satisfied until they are resolved for your sake and for the care of those who will follow.

As patients, you have a right to be well educated by your health care providers, including the right:

- To be enlightened and empowered with knowledge so your minds can be in sync with your bodies while dealing with health problems.
- To be given clear information in basic language that you can understand.
- To be shown visuals, when appropriate, to help you understand

information better.

- To be educated with current, evidence-based information that includes both the broad scope and the important details that relate to your health situation.
- To be given the opportunity to ask questions and get clear, accurate, and direct answers.
- To be offered clear and objective information as a basis for making surgery and treatment decisions.
  o When health care providers have a bias or strong recommendations about surgeries and treatments, these providers should present their recommendations within the broader scope of options and explain why they are advocating one over the others.
  o You should have the opportunity to discuss surgery and treatment options so you can make informed decisions and give consent for the procedures and treatments that you believe will work best for you.
- To be given information to support your main consultations with details about your medical problems, surgeries, treatments, tests, and drugs. You should receive this supportive information in the form of printed or electronic documents.
- To be instructed on how to be safe at all times during your care.
- To know how to contact health care providers and emergency care when necessary.
- To receive navigation information so you know how to find your way to appointments, support services, eating places, and amenities.
- To be acknowledged and empowered in your role as a partner in your care so you can effectively participate in the process of care to help achieve the best results.
- To know how to perform self-care procedures, when appropriate, to increase your independence and save visits to the medical center.
- To be offered various learning options to help you gain the knowledge you need and want.
  o These options include printed materials, website links, group sessions, and self-learning options related to your health situation.
  o You can expect that large medical centers will have more

resources and options than smaller ones.
- To know what types of support are available, and how to access this support, especially if you are dealing with major or long term health conditions.
  o This support includes social workers, counsellors, therapists, spiritual care, and community organizations.
- To have the opportunity to appropriately advocate for the needs of yourself and others.

As a current or former patient, you may feel you want to help other patients with the knowledge you gained through your experience. If you have an interest, talk to your educators or other health care providers to see if there are any opportunities. These are some of the ways you may be able to contribute:

- By offering to participate on patient advisory groups or committees to help enhance patient care.
- By telling the story of your experience to help encourage other patients. You may be able to do this at a teaching session, on a video, or as a story in a publication or on a website.
- By volunteering to be photographed or videoed to represent common patient experiences so the center can show other patients what these experiences are like.
- By offering to help in the development of printed materials and other learning options. Health care educators often need patient input to determine how to help patients learn well. You may also have the chance to help evaluate materials, programs, or websites to see how well they are being used and understood.
- By mentoring other patients with your knowledge and experience, if appropriate.
- By promoting patient learning options and encouraging other patients to take advantage of these options so they can be empowered with knowledge.

Even though you have these rights at most medical centers, keep in mind that no place of care is perfect, and you can expect to find some gaps in patient education since providing it consistently well can be a big challenge. If your safety is being compromised, then you should be clear and direct about requesting that the problem be addressed. Otherwise, taking a positive and constructive approach will be most effective.

Make requests of your health care providers. Be specific and tell them what you want to learn and how you'd like to learn it. Don't complain about anything without offering a suggested solution. You may want to write down what you see as gaps and then explain how these gaps could best be filled with certain types of learning options. Since these centers exist to serve you, they will generally take your requests seriously and do what they can to resolve issues and offer learning opportunities. Providing effective education for all types of patients is a major task that can take years to develop and implement comprehensively, so be patient with the process. Affirm the progress when you see that care providers are making efforts to address learning needs and ensure that patients are enlightened and empowered for the sake of their health.